Building Staff/Volunteer Relations

Ivan H. Scheier

Copyright © 2003 by: Energize, Inc.
5450 Wissahickon Avenue
Philadelphia, PA 19144 USA
www.energizeinc.com

ISBN 0-940576-28-7 (printed ed.)

ISBN 0-940576-31-7 (electronic ed.)
(Available from the Online Bookstore at www.energizeinc.com.)

Original edition, copyright 1993, ISBN 0-940576-14-7
Library of Congress Catalog Number 93-73624

All rights reserved. Purchasers of this book may reproduce the various checklists for use in their own volunteer programs. Otherwise, no part of this book may be reproduced in any form, or by electronic or mechanical means, including information storage and retrieval systems, without permission in writing from the publisher. This is a revised edition of *The Staff/Volunteer Relations Collection*, originally published as three separate booklets by Yellowfire Press in 1987.

Printed in the United States of America

Table of Contents

Introduction to the Revised Edition i

Introduction to the 1987 Edition ii

1 Setting the Stage 1
Organizational Receptivity to Volunteers;
History, Myth, and Diagnosis of Favoring Factors

Teamwork Checklist

2 Respecting Staff Concerns 11
Legitimate and Mythical Staff Fears about Volunteers

Perspectives On Volunteers: A Checklist for Individual Staff

3 Satisfy Staff First 27
The Job Factor Process

4 Satisfying Work for Volunteers 39
The Window of Work Process

5 Building the Team 57
Techniques for Supporting Volunteers and Staff Together

Afterword 65
'Til We Meet Again
Now That We've Met Again
2002 Update

Appendix A 69
A Starting Point for Policy Formation about Volunteers

Appendix B 71
"Titles of Caring": An Exercise to Expand the Concept of
Volunteer Involvement

Introduction to the Revised Edition

This book is about staff and volunteers enjoying their work more and therefore enjoying work with each other more. Beyond just enjoying—*appreciating*.

After a half-century of the profession of volunteer administration, could such a book still be needed? Is it conceivable that, instead of valuing volunteers, many agencies continue to patronize and trivialize them?

Yes, unfortunately. The considerable number of people who keep on buying this book presumably do so for more than historical interest. And volunteer programs are still treated as expendable "luxuries" in budget crunches, precisely the situation in which they are most needed.

So what else is new? Certainly not the principles embodied in this book. For twenty years now, I've referred to these as a "fresh approach." I hereby pledge to stop doing so. More accurately, a large number of volunteer coordinators (quite possibly a majority) haven't seriously *tried* them yet.

What, then, are the principles uniting the chapters of this book (originally published as three separate monographs)?

Staff are people, too. The success of a volunteer program depends as much on staff motivation as it does on volunteer motivation. It is not enough to accept this principle in theory; it must be rigorously applied in practice.

One implication of this is a "balance of praise" principle. You cannot form a staff/volunteer (or any other) team by praising one member of the team and not the other. All the worse if that other member ends up not just ignored but deplored. Indeed, intended or not, whenever we sanctify volunteers, we run the risk of satanizing staff. *Building Staff/Volunteer Relations* derives a number of tactics and strategies implied by this balance of praise principle. The theme, again: it is not enough to treat volunteers like staff, we must also treat staff like volunteers!

Another balance principle holds that it is just as important for staff to be happy in their work as for volunteers to be happy in their work. This is because people who are satisfied in their work are more likely to be satisfied in their *work together*. What appears to be staff and volunteers disliking *each other* may really be more that each dislike *their own work*.

Much of this book is therefore based on the premise that fulfilling work for volunteers must first assure that staff are content with their own jobs. In addition, we must try to ensure that increased staff job satisfaction is directly caused by, and traceable to, the work of volunteers.

There is an additional principle for the creation of fulfilling paid and unpaid work: *the people who do the work should design the work.* Seriously.

All the chapters embrace a "scope of responsibility" principle: essentially, the volunteer coordinator cannot do it alone—whether to ensure good staff/volunteer relations or anything else in a successful volunteer program. The entire agency, most certainly including policy-setting management, must commit to active participation.

Onward, now, from principle to practice..

Introduction to the 1987 Edition

A decade ago, my booklet "Winning with Staff' proposed some fresh approaches for dealing with staff resistance to volunteers—then the number one problem in agency-based volunteer programs. Any concern that the problem would vanish before I had a chance to write a sequel has long since been dispelled.

The challenge has, if anything, broadened. First of all, we now realize that staff need not be the oppressor" of volunteers for the problem to exist. In groups where volunteers dominate, by numbers or policy position, it is the staff person who sometimes feels thwarted by volunteers, rather than vice versa.

Finally, a related challenge can exist in groups where there are no staff at all, that is, in groups composed entirely of volunteers, such as self-help groups, service clubs, many churches or synagogues, etc. A variation of "staff resistance" occurs here when the "new kids" in the group find the "old guard" blocking significant participation.

The general case in any organization is that there are:

~ *Gatekeepers* who control access to participation, whether as staff, the chairperson of a board, the officer of a club, etc.; and

~ *Potential Participants*, paid or unpaid, seeking wider or deeper involvement in the organization.

The gatekeepers can open the gate to participation with a welcoming smile, or open it just a crack and maybe let you squeeze in (partly and uncomfortably), or slam it shut in your face.

This book is about the last two circumstances. If you're now in the first situation, I hope you won't use this book as an excuse to go looking for problems on which to apply your shiny new techniques. Instead, enjoy, and use these strategies to prevent deterioration in participation paradise. Know, too, that however comfortable the situation is at home, your people are probably going to encounter blockages to participation in other organizations they deal with.

For the rest, every situation is different. Therefore, this book is essentially a selection of concepts and strategies from which you can choose according to your individual needs and style.

I do hope, however, you'll read it through at least once before beginning to make such decisions. There's a certain logic in the sequence of presentation.

Good luck.

Setting the Stage

A Rough-and-Ready History

If I ever try to write a Bible of human services, I know what the first sentence will be:

In the beginning there were volunteers.

I'm having trouble with the second sentence, but let that pass. In the beginning there were volunteers. Every human service occupation or profession has volunteers in its ancestry. The first social workers were volunteers; the first teachers; the first nurses and other health care workers. Firefighters were originally volunteers, and still today, about 80% of the fire departments in the U.S. are volunteer. Early clergy weren't paid and many still aren't today (or anyway, not much). There's an old Judaic tradition that the Rabbi never accepts money for his services from the Congregation; he supports his family by taking other jobs.

In the beginning, police officers were volunteers, and much of law enforcement is still done on that basis. Elected officials were at first unpaid and that still occurs in some cases today, especially in smaller communities. The entire concept of probation, employing thousands today, originated in 1841. John Augustus, the world's first probation officer, was a volunteer. Early child care workers were unpaid; they were called "parents."

And on and on. In the beginning there were only volunteers and they pioneered all the paid positions in human services today.[1]

Sometime quite early in the last century, the pendulum began to swing away from all-volunteer human services toward paid personnel to replace volunteers. The irony is that while many worry today about volunteers replacing staff, historically the process has always been precisely the reverse: staff replacing volunteers.

Why did the pendulum move towards increasing proportions of paid staff? Once volunteers established the need for a service, and there was growing demand for it (especially in more densely populated areas), we needed people on the job for longer and longer hours. Then, as now, the person who can volunteer full-time is rare. At the same time, we started asking people to lock themselves in to large portions of time and money for preparatory professional education—something volunteers are unlikely to do in their spare time. Thus, a professional helping class (mainly paid) began to emerge and, by mid-century or so, it looked like volunteerism would soon be obsolete.

But the obituaries were premature. What some then saw as an amiable relic from an earlier age of horse-and-buggy helping not only hung on, but experienced a vital renewal. The reasons are worth a book in itself. Probably, agencies without volunteers began to feel a little lonely, and dangerously isolated from their communities. They also realized that a thin line of staff could never alone meet all the needs of their clients.

So the pendulum which had swung first from all-volunteer to nearly all paid staff, finally edged back again to somewhere in the middle—significant numbers of both volunteers and staff in the human service delivery system. It's been oscillating there ever since the 1960's, give or take a decade, depending on which service area you're talking about. This oscillation is all too often uneasy, adversarial in tone, when it could be mutually supportive. Thus, we need to get back to the kind of meaningful volunteer job assignment which permits this year's volunteer job to be next year's new paid position. Then volunteers can go on to pioneer other positions.

There are certain fundamental lessons this history can teach us:

~ It's difficult or impossible to do the job with just volunteers.

~ It's equally difficult or impossible to do the job just with paid staff.

Therefore, we're going to have to find the right *mixture* of staff and volunteers, and make it *work*. That's what this book is about—and nobody is telling you it will be easy. The co-existence of volunteers and staff in human service agencies is, with a few shining exceptions, like a marriage that hasn't settled down yet, after 25 years! But, for sure, the honeymoon is over.

Time now for realism, rather than romance.

What Doesn't Work (Usually)

Without meaning to tease, it's probably useful to get out of the way a few things that don't work, and never have. It seems silly to waste time trying them over and over. Maybe that's a trifle overstated. These three approaches have hardly ever worked in the last thirty years: inspirational intimidation; psychologizing the situation; and rubbing on a little training. A fourth loser is separatism and is dealt with in "The Search for Common Ground" in Chapter 5.

Anyhow, with these out of the way, we can stop making the same old mistakes over and over, and go on to making some creative new ones.

Inspirational Intimidation

We admire our wonderful volunteers so much. It pains us when others greet righteous enthusiasm with indifference or disdain. We're prone to overreact with over-sell. What comes out then—as well as at most every annual volunteer recognition event—is anecdotes suggesting that all volunteers are either "Miracle Workers" or "Brilliant Amateurs" or "Achievers of Incredible Results as If by Magic."

We mean well, but see how such statements can come across to skeptical staff:

Miracle Worker - Sounds like a rescue operation. Nobody likes to be seen as needing to be rescued.

Brilliant Amateurs - I once heard this prideful announcement by a volunteer: "The theories said this kid could never learn to read. But I didn't know about all the theories, and I never studied any textbooks on it. *So*, I just went ahead and taught him to read."

Scattered applause I didn't join. I wanted both hands free to strangle the guy. Because what came across was that all staff's struggle and expense of getting professional training and experience wasn't worth a thing. Why can't we upgrade volunteers without downgrading all that staff stands for?

Get Incredible Results as If by Magic - Magic shows are great to watch—from a distance. But I'm not sure I'd want to work up close to a magician—my job might disappear!

These kinds of implications are almost always unintentional, but no less insulting to staff, for that reason. They also ultimately do a disservice to volunteers by setting up unrealistic expectations for their performance—a "set-up" in more than one sense.

If you must miracle-ize volunteers, at least tell a few counterpart stories about exemplary staff (there almost always are such stories if you look for them). Better yet, regale with anecdotes about the great achievements of staff-volunteer teams. Praise the partnership. Best of all, prevent inspirational intimidation of staff by emphasizing that volunteers, by and large, are just decent folks who want to help out. Helpful human beings are much more satisfying as co-workers than saintly wizards.

Psychologizing the Situation

One of the hardest things to do is respect staff skeptics, realizing and believing that, though we regret their "resistance" to volunteers, they may still be fine people and good, caring staff. That's not only the ethical position to take; it's often a fully truthful one and frequently effective as well. People see you as someone they can talk to and negotiate with, rather than as an implacable fanatic on the subject of volunteers.

On the other hand, it is terribly tempting to ascribe a staff person's skepticism to basic defects in character or problems in mental health. The insinuations are almost always unintentional, but they are there.

Please watch, for example, the use of clinically-connected terms and phrases such as staff are "threatened by," "anxious about," or "paranoid" about volunteers. I know you don't really mean to suggest that the origin of staff failure to support volunteers is because they hated their mothers, or vice versa. But unfortunately that kind of concept can easily insinuate itself in otherwise productive dialogue.

There are several problems with psychologizing the staff-volunteer relational issue. First, such statements are very often untrue, unfair and misleading. Even where grains of truth may exist, performing psychoanalysis or the like on all affected staff (or volunteers) is impractically expensive and time-consuming! Also, psychodynamic finger-pointing at staff naturally provokes a retaliatory finger pointed right back at you. Thus, it may well account for the equally absurd legend of the neurotic volunteer.

To be sure, there are some volunteers who may have mental problems. Indeed, there are some organizations you have to be crazy to volunteer for. There are also some staff who are neurotic, at least some of the time. But that's not the point. Neither staff nor volunteers are predominantly neurotic or psychotic. Therefore, that's

Chapter 1: Setting the Stage

not the general issue we're dealing with in staff-volunteer relations. Unless you're into name-calling under cover of psychology.

Let's Just Rub on a Little Training

Most of us no longer believe in panaceas; formal learning may be the last surviving snake oil. Suspiciously often, at foggy crossroads in our lives, we go back to school and get another degree. And if there's a problem at the agency, a favorite quick fix is to hire a trainer, have a workshop, and move right on to something else.

Similarly, some seem to believe that mandatory staff training in the use of volunteers will make resistance magically disappear. I doubt it, as a rule. The kinds of strategies we're talking about in this book spread far beyond the time confines of a workshop. Besides, there's no such thing as education without motivation.

A case in point: I used to volunteer with juvenile delinquent boys who were school dropouts or kick-outs. At first I suffered from the prevailing prejudice that these boys actually weren't too smart.

Then it came time for them to take the written test for becoming licensed automobile drivers. One and all blew that test out of the water, with scores ranging from 90% on up (far better than I did with my finely honed test-taking skills fresh from graduate school). Why? These boys desperately wanted to drive a car (with a slight preference that it be done on a legal basis). Therefore, they readily absorbed the necessary material. Unfortunately, no teacher had ever been able to get through to them that things like English and math were nearly as important as driving a car.

The case is parallel for "training out" staff resistance to volunteers and "training in" support for same. You can sit staff down in a classroom and give them great information on how to involve and supervise volunteers, but if they don't see any gripping reason for learning the material, they won't even hear it. Certainly, training staff in how to work with volunteers can be a useful auxiliary tactic if, at the same time, other approaches described in this book are building staff motivation to learn the material.

And while we're at it, orientation of volunteers is at least equally important for assuring good staff-volunteer relations. Strongly recommended here is a deliberate, well-planned session on "the care and feeding of staff." From the very beginning, be sure volunteers understand that a primary part of their job is to make staff's job easier by providing relevant sympathy and support. Let staff themselves handle some of the sessions on this, sharing, for example, insights on why they're sometimes grouchy (it isn't because they hate volunteers) or maybe don't always answer telephone calls promptly (it isn't because they think volunteers are unimportant; it's because the ceiling just fell down). Whether directly involved in this sensitizing training or not, staff will probably appreciate your making efforts to orient volunteers in this way.

Too few volunteer programs make such an effort at representing the staff perspective as a significant, self-conscious part of volunteer orientation and training. A spot poll suggests maybe one in thirty programs do. This may be just another consequence of a secret assumption that staff resistance to volunteers is their problem. They must change their ways; we needn't change ours. Yet, the best way to get a smile is to give one and not expect staff to produce them out of thin air. And, generally, the best way to earn support is to offer it. We volunteer people need to think about that.

Building Staff/Volunteer Relations © 2003 Energize, Inc.

Diagnosis as a Basis for Action

How do you know when you have a problem in staff-volunteer relations?

On the one hand, don't go looking for trouble where none exists. On the other hand, don't wait to be hit on the head with a two-by-four before reacting. Thus, don't assume everything's okay unless you see staff and volunteers actually punching each other out. That's actually happened, but only once that I know of in thirty years.

Look for subtler signs from staff. It's not so much active sabotage as passive resistance; it's not so much what staff does as what they don't do. Don't expect snarls, but worry at the absence of smiles. Staff may not overtly "bad mouth" volunteers but they may fail to show up at volunteer recognition events. Visible hassling of volunteers is a far less likely sign than sheer absence of staff requests for volunteers in meaningful work.

Finally, it's not so much that staff hate volunteers as that they have other more important priorities. Hating volunteers today is something like hating motherhood, God, and the right to boo the home team. You don't directly challenge such conventionally sacred values; you just ignore or trivialize them by putting your time elsewhere.

Sometimes, the conflict of loyalties is more objective. I was once consulted on a case of token volunteerism at a children's institution. The superintendent seemed genuinely interested in changing that for the better. But he showed me two memos from the top boss. One said, in effect, "volunteers are operational priority #1 in this system," but there were no positive or negative sanctions to back up this statement. The other memo said something like this: "Form X-870-B2 is not being properly completed by staff. Unless this is promptly remedied, we will be unable to process paychecks in the new fiscal year." To which memo do you think the superintendent—and the staff—gave priority?

So much for diagnosis from the staff side. On the volunteer side, signs of a staff-volunteer problem are relatively more straightforward: volunteers start dropping out all over the place.

Organizational Receptivity to Volunteers

In addition to significant signals from staff and from volunteers, there is a third basis for deciding where you stand on staff-volunteer relations: organizational climate and receptivity.

At the end of this chapter is a "Teamwork Checklist" designed to help you diagnose your own organizational situation carefully, identify and capitalize on strengths, raise awareness on issues and challenges, and launch positive planning to do something about current problem areas. The questions themselves may help respondents discover the scope and depth of issues related to volunteers. The chapters that follow will give you some strategies for making the changes necessary to help your organization score even higher.

Before using the checklist, consider changing some of the more abstract terms to more concrete, relevant ones. Thus, "the overall organization or agency" in Checklist Statement #1 might be changed to the name of your agency or organization. "Top management" in Statement #2 might be similarly specified for your agency, and so on for other statements. You should also feel free to add or delete statements, according to their relevance for your organization.

Select several different people to fill out the checklist, independently of each other. Representation should include the person most directly responsible for the volunteer program (one hopes this is a professional volunteer coordinator or director), a volunteer or two, one line staff person who works with volunteers, and one who does not. Wherever anonymity can encourage candor, it should be offered as an option.

Ideally the checklist will also be completed by at least one middle management and one top management person. In any case, management should be involved in discussion of results and receive a report on outcomes. Remember here that some of the statements probably represent areas management has never really thought about in connection with the volunteer program. The whole process can be educational.

Using Checklist Results

Once the checklist has been administered, convene a group to compare and discuss results. The group should include all those who completed the checklist, plus others selected on a need-to-know basis.

Now compare responses statement by statement among those who complete the checklist. You may want first of all to discuss and clarify your understanding of what each statement means. (Many are treated throughout this book.)

Then, consider first the case where *solid consensus* exists among strengths (high scores) in your staff/volunteer situation. These factors can be pretty much left alone for now, though a review of "what are we doing right here?" could be helpful in preserving the happy state of affairs. Complacency is certainly not recommended.

Otherwise, planning for improvement of staff/volunteer relations should focus on those statements which consensus rated as low, insofar as they indicate factors on which: we agree positive change is desirable; and such change is reasonably within the capability of planners. Thus, if discussants concur that the agency does not have an effective policy statement on volunteers (checklist statement #2), and further agree that such a policy is needed, they can recommend or actually launch development of appropriate agency guidelines.

Indeed, *virtually every checklist statement is a nucleus around which a volunteer program policy statement can be developed.* The only exceptions are checklist statements #1 and possibly #11 as well. A policy on volunteers is high priority for agencies seriously interested in cultivating volunteer support. This policy should be clear, realistic, specific, in writing and widely disseminated throughout the agency. As implemented, it will prevent all the damage ambiguity can do to a volunteer program, and also deter willful misunderstanding of the organization's commitment to volunteer involvement. There should be wide agency participation in formulation of the volunteer program policy. (To help you in further consideration of policy statements, Appendix A provides a "Starting Point" list of possible items to include.)

Lack of consensus on a checklist statement is valuable when it triggers clarifying and productive discussion. Thus, if management thinks that goals for increased numbers of volunteers are realistic (#8), while the volunteer coordinator and line staff feel these goals are too high, we have something about which we need to communicate better. More realistic numerical targets could well result from clarification, information exchange, and negotiation.

Here and throughout the checklist, one is struck by the extent to which top management must be involved in key decisions affecting the volunteer program. Indeed, top management is often the only place where such decisions can finally be made. How different this is from the token theory of top management involvement: show up once a year at the volunteer recognition event; symbolically put your arm around volunteers; breathe a sigh of relief, and opt out of the process until next year at the same time.

An excellent book describing how top management must opt in is *From the Top Down: The Executive Role in Volunteer Program Success* by Susan J. Ellis (Philadelphia: Energize, 1996).

Another sometimes useful datum is the total Teamwork Checklist score, ranging from zero to 100. Once again, dramatic differences among checklist raters can lead to illuminating discussion, such as if top management gives the staff/volunteer situation higher scores on the checklist than the volunteer coordinator does. The two are seeing different things and need to share their perceptions; it is unlikely both are right.

But where there is at least nominal overall agreement among raters on total checklist scores, this score has significance approximately as follows:

81-100= Very Good to Excellent. There's little more you can do to improve this situation. But beware of complacency, and doublecheck that the high score wasn't produced by overly optimistic or uninformed raters.

56-80= Good to Very Good. Still, good isn't perfect. There's room for improvement.

36-55= Fair to Average. There is definitely room for improvement. At least some factors in the overall situation are probably seriously hurting your program.

16-35= Poor to Fair. Immediate and decisive attack on the problem is a high priority.

0-15= Very Poor. Don't give up without trying, but ring all the alarm bells and mobilize for action. A very low score is not necessarily cause for despair. In part, it may mean your volunteer program is relatively new and conditions for good volunteer-staff relations have not yet been set up. Or it may simply mean that many of the factors are not yet fully understood or known by you.

Certain of the individual statement ratings can also be especially revealing of the overall situation. Thus, statement #1 is a stopper. Consensus on a low score suggests that somehow volunteers are expected to rescue a seriously ailing organization. It usually doesn't work that way. In fact, quite the reverse: a deeply troubled agency will almost certainly destroy its own volunteer program or never allow the program to develop properly in the first place, before that volunteer program ever "rescues" the organization.

It is generally accepted that checklist statement #1 is the top priority and foundation for both volunteer program and staff. Past checklist users have also commented that if checklist factors #1, #2, and #3 are in place, everything else will follow. To this, I would add: until factor #1 is in place, other factors are unlikely to follow, or mean much if they do follow.

I suggest you re-administer the checklist every three to six months to gauge progress, spot new problems early, and re-stimulate the problem-solving process.

Next Steps

The next chapter introduces some of the major concerns expressed by staff about volunteers and gives you reasonable, concrete ways to respond. Then we will spend some time on one of the most critical areas of volunteer program success: the design of work. First we'll examine staff work satisfaction and then volunteer job development. Finally, we'll consider active ways to support staff/volunteer teamwork.

It should be mentioned that, in recent years, the volunteer field has been advised to limit its use of the word "job" in relation to volunteers. Some lawsuits (though quite rare) have attempted to claim back wages for time spent in a "volunteer job," on the grounds that the work was something that should have been done by an employee. In reaction, some attorneys recommend making a clear delineation between jobs (paid) and what we call the work we ask volunteers to do. So terms such as "volunteer position" or "volunteer assignment" are now seen more regularly. Of course, semantic acrobatics aside, we are still talking about work to be done! If your agency prefers that you do not use the term "job" for volunteers, just substitute your word of choice as you read the rest of this book.

---

[1] For a complete history of the impact volunteers have had on American society, see *By the People: A History of Americans as Volunteers, Third Edition*, by Susan J. Ellis and Katherine Noyes Campbell (Philadelphia: Energize, 2004).

Teamwork Checklist
Staff and Volunteers

Date: _____

Name (*Optional*): _____

Role in Organization: _____

Relationship to Volunteer Program: _____

Listed below are some key factors affecting the state of staff/volunteer relations in an agency-sponsored volunteer program. Please rate each of these statements on the following scale for the volunteer program with which you are associated in this organization.

5 = Absolutely: things are excellent
4 = Most of the time (very good)
3 = At least half of the time (good)
2 = Occasionally (fair)
1 = Rarely (poor)
0 = Never (very poor) or unknown (because if you don't know about it, it can't be much of a factor)

Ratings

1. Our overall organization or agency is stable, healthy, and free of serious conflict and basic survival anxiety.

    _____

2. The top management of this organization has developed and effectively comunicated a policy on volunteers which is clear, specific, well-informed, positive, and has teeth in it.

    _____

3. Roles of staff and volunteers are clearly defined both generically and in terms of specific tasks.

    _____

4. Volunteers are clearly perceived by everyone as either a direct or indirect support for staff and the organization as a whole. Volunteers are not seen as a means of replacing staff.

    _____

5. Most volunteer job descriptions are directly based on staff needs for assistance in their work. Information about these needs is provided by staff themselves as specific things which are inefficient or unnecessary for paid staff to do or as additional things they can accomplish with volunteer help.

    _____

6. We have a wide variety of volunteer jobs and roles from which staff may select those with which they are most comfortable. Staff members actively participate in developing this wide range of volunteer job designs.

    _____

7. Staff have solid ownership of the volunteer program via their participation in planning, recruiting, screening, job design, orientation and training, supervision, and evaluation of volunteers. (Volunteers can be fired and staff know it.) This staff participation involves both policy-setting and whatever program implementation staff have time for.

    _____

8. The targets for increased numbers of volunteers are realistic. We do not play the numbers game here with our volunteer program.

    _____

Building Staff/Volunteer Relations

© 2003 Energize, Inc.

9. A significant, well-planned part of orientation and training for volunteers emphasizes sensitivity and sympathy to staff problems and the primary importance of being supportive to staff. _____

10. Wherever possible (and this means frequently), volunteers are recognized and rewarded in conjunction with their staff supervisors or associates. That is, the recognition goes to a staff-volunteer team or partnership. _____

11. Volunteers regularly choose and publicly commend staff people they consider outstanding; for example, "the staff person of the month." _____

12. Our organization consistently implements a system of concrete, specific rewards for staff who work effectively with volunteers. The need for mobilizing community volunteer support to achieve organizational or job goals is built into every staff job description. _____

13. A staff person's performance with volunteers is regularly evaluated and seriously considered in decisions concerning that person's status and promotion in the organization. _____

14. Individual staff receptivity to volunteers is carefully assessed. With rare exceptions, volunteers are first assigned to more receptive staff who are also knowledgeable about working with volunteers. _____

15. Experience working with volunteers, openness to delegating meaningful duties to them, and creative belief in their potential are criteria actively used in recruiting and selecting new staff at all levels in the organization. _____

16. We regularly conduct both pre- and in-service orientation and training programs for staff on how to work effectively with volunteers. This training is carefully planned, and sufficient time is allowed for it. _____

17. A well-qualified person has been designated to coordinate/direct the volunteer program and act as a bridge linking staff and volunteers. This person is allowed enough time to do the job properly. _____

18. The above-described volunteer coordinator position is at management level. The coordinator has ample opportunity to participate in organizational decision-making, particularly as it might affect the volunteer program. _____

19. The volunteer program office is conveniently located and easily accessible to both staff and volunteers. _____

20. We have effective grievance mechanisms for handling staff/volunteer problems. These mechanisms are available to both volunteers and staff. _____

TOTAL SUM _____

Building Staff/Volunteer Relations

© 2003 Energize, Inc.

2 Respecting Staff Concerns

Frank Miller Talks Straight from the Shoulder

A number of years ago I participated in a workshop on the topic of staff-volunteer relations. There was some concern that here we were, as usual, the convinced talking to the convinced. No one in the room represented whom we were really talking about—the sincerely skeptical staff person.

So we went out and found Frank Miller who kindly consented to share his honest doubts about volunteers, provided only that we didn't lynch him for it. We didn't, but the discussion did get a bit lively at times. The following is taken from handwritten notes on Frank's talk. The writing wavers in spots, and in other places some small splashes of liquid appear to have blurred the manuscript. But, generally, this is the gist of it, according to my best recollection:

> Hi. Good morning. I'm sure glad to be here with all you volunteers.
>
> First off I don't want you to think I dislike volunteers. While I've always been too busy for it myself I still think volunteers are real nice people who mean well. Heck, my mother volunteered a lot and my wife Mary does her volunteer work every Tuesday, when she's not needed at home. I think it's great; gives her a chance to get out of the house. Even my daughter Sheila volunteers summers in the junior program, until she's old enough to get a real job.
>
> The other thing you should know about me is that I've been in the Social Work profession for 25 years now, and due to retire in three or four years. The agency has thought well enough of my work to promote me to Deputy Director.
>
> Having said that, I want to follow Ivan Scheier's instructions to this effect: whatever else you do, Mr. Miller, be Frank.
>
> So here I am, Frank Miller, sharing some candid concerns about volunteers in our agency. First of all, I'm deeply proud of the tradition of excellence in our agency. We want the very best for our clients—not second best—and always have felt that way. Among other things, that means the highest professional standards backed by the best possible training and education for all our staff.
>
> For this reason, a dozen years ago we instituted a policy of

Building Staff/Volunteer Relations © 2003 Energize, Inc.

Chapter 2: Respecting Staff Concerns

requiring MSWs for all new professional employees. I had only a Bachelor's Degree at the time and could have grandfathered in on this requirement but, both ethically and professionally, I thought the policy so important that I decided to take it as a requirement for myself. That meant six long years of night school, arduous and expensive, to get that MSW, I don't mind telling you that I very much missed spending that time with Mary and the kids.

Now—after all that struggle on behalf of principle and on behalf of clients—you folks seem to be telling me that any amateur can walk in off the street and do my job! And you wonder why I'm upset! You're violating a crucial commitment to education as a cornerstone of excellence in my profession, and an assurance of quality care for clients.

Education aside, you know the old saying: "You get what you pay for." Among other things, that means reasonable reliability. Remember, volunteering is, well, voluntary. Volunteers can come and go as they please, take vacations whenever. If they happen to feel like doing what you ask them to do, fine. But what if they don't? In short, it's practically their right to be unreliable. Is that the way to help clients who've had plenty of uncertainty in their lives already? Indeed, is that the way to help me as a staff person?

Yes, how about me? I hope you don't mind my being a little selfish about this. You keep insisting that volunteers are an investment, not a gift, that I have to put in a lot of time and effort supervising them (or risk having a lot of loose cannons running around!). Great! I've already got a caseload of 60 clients. Now you want me to add a caseload of 20 volunteers! I really don't need that extra responsibility. It's a paradox, that's what it is. I'm supposed to need volunteers because I'm overloaded, so you assign me volunteers which increase my load further. No thanks. It's easier to do it myself.

We have a solemn ethical and legal obligation to maintain absolute confidentiality on all sensitive material relating to our clients. Our relatively small staff of six exercises constant vigilance to ensure total compliance with this obligation. But add a bunch of volunteers not steeped in the crucial need for confidentiality and the circle of knowledge grows to, say, 100. Somewhere, there's bound to be leaks. Do we really have the right to take such grave risks with our clients' right to privacy? I think not.

Speaking of privacy, the agency as a whole has some rights in that regard, too. I'm darned uncomfortable about a bunch of naive non-professionals, however well-meaning, looking over our shoulders, not really understanding what we're doing or why. Then babbling misinterpretations all over town. Including to the media.

And here I go being "selfish" again. I chose this career, knowing full well I might make more money somewhere else. I chose it because it was work I felt important to do. Still, a family man has to have some concern for financial security; I hope you can understand that.

Chapter 2: Respecting Staff Concerns

> *Let's face it. The more volunteers you get, the better excuse decision-makers have to cut your budget, or fail to restore it. You go in asking for a decent budget and they'll say: "Heck, you don't need all that money. Go out and get more volunteers instead." Don't deny it; I've heard it, and so have you, probably. And I'll bet you've also heard, as I have, politicians praising volunteers because of all the money they save—money the politicians can now put into things rather than people. So, though maybe you don't mean it that way, volunteers are in fact a direct threat to the modest financial security I do have, including the pension I'm desperately counting on in a few years. I'd like to leave thinking the agency is in reasonably good financial shape, too.*
>
> *All in all I think volunteers are nice, well-meaning people, who as a group were great before we had fully developed professional services. In fact, they were all we had then. Today, they're just a throwback which fundamentally threatens that hard-won professionalism.*

[Applause? Groans? Screams? Reasoned, Caring Discussion?]

All right... there is no Frank Miller, per se. There are many of him. And many Frances Millers, too. They are real, and Frank's speech can help us respond to that reality in several important ways.

Dealing Directly with Staff Concerns

As Frank Miller has already done, staff tend to express one or more of four main fears about volunteers:

~ Volunteers will take too much time and will become an additional burden rather than a help.

~ One can never get rid of volunteers, even when they can't or won't do their jobs.

~ Volunteers pose a threat to confidentiality.

~ Volunteers will take jobs away from employees, and/or be used as justification for a reduced budget.

Some are relieved when staff don't express these concerns. But if, in fact, staff do worry about these things and won't publicly discuss them, you've got real problems, namely with festering feelings. I'm even suggesting you take the initiative in raising these issues (*see note below), just to be sure they aren't lurking around beneath the

---

*Here is one more idea for an exercise: Have someone "deliver" Frank Miller's speech (or an adaptation of it that applies directly to your setting) to an audience of staff or other trainees. This can be a powerful roleplay either for introducing issues at the beginning of a workshop, or for practicing productive strategies to address these issues, at the end of such a workshop. Watch for, and confront, sheer anger and cruel caricature, in lieu of caring discussion.

Building Staff/Volunteer Relations © 2003 Energize, Inc.

Chapter 2: Respecting Staff Concerns

surface. If they aren't of real concern to staff, no harm done. And, generally, such an initiative shows you have confidence enough in the volunteer program to deal realistically and effectively with potential difficulties, rather than hiding behind monolithic conviction.

The other danger is in assuming that expressed staff concerns are simply hypocritical excuses for footdragging. It's far better to assume sincerity until proven otherwise. In fact, the main staff fears about volunteers are perfectly consistent with origins in a sensitive, intelligent staff person who genuinely cares about the well-being of clients and agency. Only after you have responded honestly and completely to staff questions—several times—and you still get the same questions as if you'd never replied to them—only then can you begin to suspect a different kettle of fish. Red herrings, to be exact.

The next four sections explore these four realistic fears, and why staff need to be afraid no longer (we hope).

Getting a Good Return on Investment in Volunteers

"It's easier to do it myself' is a death sentence for a volunteer program, when pronounced by staff who sincerely believe it. The point is plausible enough until we demonstrate efficient strategies for staff coming out clearly ahead in time returned by volunteers compared to time invested in them.

To begin, acknowledge that yes, volunteers take staff time. Particularly in the early stages of program planning and implementation, staff might be putting in an hour or two for every hour of volunteer time they get back. That's to be expected. But when things settle down, you should normally expect to get back at least 10 to 15 hours of work from volunteers for every hour you invest in them. In some programs, the payoff can get as high as 100 to 1 or even 200 to 1. There are some studies supporting this conclusion. And this doesn't even consider the case of the specialist volunteer who does what staff could never do no matter how much time staff invested!

Here are eight things that might help staff improve its input-output time efficiency with volunteers:

1. Careful recruiting, screening and placement of volunteers in the first place. A small, quality effort is far more efficient than a large "revolving door" program in response to "numbers game" pressure (ususally from top administration). Hand-picked and hand-placed volunteers are the way to go, via "each-one-reach-one" recruiting by outstanding current volunteers or by staff. Such volunteers are more likely to take care of themselves, less likely to be leavers or losers.

2. Place a good proportion of your volunteers in jobs which are time-saving for staff, rather than time-absorbing. Applying a staff "Job Factor" (which we'll describe in Chapter 3) should turn up lots of possibilities here.

3. Generally, volunteers will take far less supervisory time when assigned work for which they already have the competence and motivation. Here is another case where taking a little more time at the front end can save tons of time later on. So, insofar as possible, place volunteers in work for which they are self-directed and already capable. The same point applies to finding groups

Chapter 2: Respecting Staff Cor

to do their pet project for you. A good, practical process to identify which volunteers are naturally suited is described in Chapter 4 "Window of Work."

4. No matter how self-directed a volunteer may be, some pre-service orientation will be needed. The rule is: taking time for thorough orientation and training beforehand will save much more time later, by clearing up unnecessary misunderstanding.

5. Where feasible logistically, group supervision of volunteers saves staff time.

6. Volunteers can often provide for one another much of the support and information they would otherwise need to get from staff. Therefore, consider investing some effort in developing support systems and networks among your volunteers

7. You can accomplish a similar thing somewhat more hierarchically by developing a buddy or mentoring system, matching good experienced volunteers with neophytes. Generally, qualified volunteers can serve as leaders/supervisors of other volunteers, ultimately accountable directly to staff in their leadership role. The volunteer leader role is also a legitimate way of providing a "career ladder" in volunteering for those who may want that. So look to volunteers to supervise other volunteers, wherever possible.

8. Often, a staff time-draining situation is not attributable to most volunteers, but only to one or a very few. So, if a volunteer persists in taking an inordinate amount of your time, and this problem doesn't occur with your other volunteers, you might have a situation in which the best way to save time is fire the volunteer. Either that or place the person in another job and/or with another staff supervisor where the prospects are better for coming out ahead time-wise.

Fire Control

The staff haunt, sometimes verbalized, sometimes repressed, goes something like this: "The thing about volunteers is that you can't order them to do anything and you can't threaten them with loss of pay. Worst of all, you can't even fire them, when all else fails. Talk about loose cannon!" Like it or not, orders and threats are common ways of "managing" employees. The perks we give to volunteers sometimes look suspiciously like "do as you damn well please." Assuring staff that they can fire volunteers, and providing clear guidelines and procedures for so doing, is the major remedy recommended.

From the very beginning, in all volunteer program policy statements, volunteer supervision guidelines, and orientation materials, make it crystal clear to volunteers and staff that a volunteer's services can be terminated for cause. The philosophy behind this should be publicly stated and goes like this:

Building Staff/Volunteer Relations © 2003 Energize, Inc.

Our bottom line is the best possible service for our clients (audience, consumers). Therefore, it's irrelevant whether you're paid or not; we expect high standards of performance in your assigned work and will give you the best support and supervision we can. To that end, if your work still isn't up to necessary standards, we reserve the absolute right to terminate your service, or re-assign you to some other more suitable work. EXACTLY AS WE DO FOR PAID STAFF

It's much easier if this policy is completely clear, from a volunteer's very earliest contact with the organization. Insofar as feasible, the following strategies will minimize the number of times the painful process of firing a volunteer will be necessary.

~ Selective, targeted volunteer recruiting, and careful, sensitive matching to volunteer jobs in the first place, will reduce the number of times it becomes necessary to fire volunteers later. The number of volunteers needing to be fired goes up directly with slapdash recruiting and mismatching. The numbers game is mainly what gets you into the termination game.

~ Emphasize the termination policy described above in orientation, training, and supervision of all volunteers.

~ The orientation and training itself should be realistic enough so that people you might otherwise have to fire later can screen themselves out early on.

~ Ditto, in orientation and training and supervision of all staff.

~ Wherever possible, volunteers should initially be given only provisional or probationary appointments, and/or a time-limited term of service. At all costs, avoid open-ended appointments-for-eternity. And where feasible, don't promise volunteers any involvement with your agency until they have successfully completed orientation and training.

The point of all this is that the more careful we are at the front end, the less misery we can expect at the other end. Give volunteers all the honorable exits you can, before the exit doors close.

So far, the significance has been mainly in prevention of the need to fire volunteers. We now move to something more like preparation for the possibility of having to fire a volunteer. The principal component here is regular, relevant feedback to the volunteer, largely as an integral part of supervision by staff but also from peers.

Failure to provide such feedback is grossly unfair to the volunteer for two main reasons. First, some of the feedback will be positive and encouraging. But whether congratulatory or cautionary, all of it will be useful to the volunteer, and s/he deserves to be treated as an adult in this respect.

Second, where inadequacies in the volunteer's work are identified and discussed, along with reasonable suggestions on improvement, the volunteer is given a fair chance to correct the problems. The worst experience I ever had as a volunteer was when a respected staff supervisor suddenly turned cold and distant and never said why. (It was 20 degrees below zero in July.) When, finally, I went to him and almost begged to be told what was wrong, it proved to be something we could deal with quite

Chapter 2: Respecting Staff Concerns

easily. He—like many staff—had just felt guilty about criticizing anyone "nice enough to volunteer." I, on the other hand, was less interested in being nice than in being effective and respected. It was therefore far worse for me when he didn't give me a chance to remove the problem that was bugging him. This point needs to be impressed on staff supervisors of volunteers.

After "prevention of" and "preparation for" firing, we come to "execution"—an unfortunate phrase, perhaps, in this context, and so is "termination"!

Let's say a volunteer has on several occasions had caring, cautionary feedback with good suggestions on how to deal with the problem(s), and time to do so. But s/he hasn't. Move now, if you haven't already, towards establishing a consensus on the need for termination. This could be via a volunteer personnel committee, preferably including volunteers themselves. You owe it to yourself and to the volunteer to be sure your fault-finding isn't biased, even unconsciously. Besides, consensus sends a firmer, more powerful message, when that is needed.

When you—or the committee—finally have to talk to the volunteer, you'll often have one great advantage over the employer of paid personnel. You can sometimes offer the volunteer another job within the organization, better shaped to his or her strong points, and more carefully avoiding weaknesses. This might still be a responsible job, not a downgrade. In any case, if the volunteer declines this offered job, it is more like him or her saying no to the agency than the agency rejecting the volunteer. If another job within the agency is not feasible, you might still be able to find a more appropriate position with some other organization in town. Your local Volunteer Center, RSVP, or volunteer leadership professional association can help here.

This point in the process is where you may first begin to suspect that the volunteer is actually more relieved than anything else. Many people know deep down that the job wasn't right for them, are as unhappy as you are about their poor performance and, consciously or not, are glad to have you take them off the hook. Sometimes this will be so, though not always.

But in any event we're getting near the end of the line in the firing process. Do not avoid an exit interview. However painful the prospect, the pain inflicted on both sides by lingering misunderstanding will be worse. One hopes this exit interview will have the character of counseling; a respectful, sensitive search for mutual understanding and support. By all means, the volunteer should be giving you as much feedback as you are giving him or her; s/he deserves that respect and you deserve that information. Wherever feasible, too, the separation should probably be billed as a resignation rather than a firing—similar to a courtesy sometimes extended to paid employees.

But it's likely to be painful still, no getting around it. Have you ever had to fire a paid employee?

In case you still believe it's never fair to fire a volunteer we attach for your consideration a letter recently recovered by staff supervisor Frank Miller, whom we've already met. (See next page.) Apparently, volunteer Viola wrote it on agency stationery but failed to put sufficient postage on it, and it somehow ended up in Frank's in-box.

Thankfully, there aren't many Violas, but one would be enough, or anything like one. Use this letter as a discussion exercise for volunteers, maybe for staff as well. Have some volunteers write a much more positive letter—they can, you know, and most would want to. Finally, why not start a correspondence between Viola and Frank Miller? Or between Viola and a volunteers-can-do-no-wrong coordinator of volunteers?

Building Staff/Volunteer Relations © 2003 Energize, Inc.

Chapter 2: Respecting Staff Concerns

Dear Prudence,

Thought I'd try to find something useful to do by writing you, while putting in my volunteer time here. They had some things for me to do today but nothing particularly interesting. That's what they're paid to do, after all.

There's lots of talk about professionalism around here. Yet between us, I'm sure I can do anything staff can do, even though I don't have a social work degree. (Maybe I can do some things better because I'm not tied up in knots by all the theory and ten syllable words!)

Anyhow, the only difference is that I don't get paid for the work, and they do. Truthfully, I get upset sometimes watching staff goof off while pulling down fat salaries. You ought to see them. They sure put in a lot of time at the water cooler, with rest room breaks every fifteen minutes, it seems. Honestly, you wouldn't believe how often they're not at their desks, or out of the office entirely, while I do their work for them.

What we need is a few more volunteers around here; save the taxpayers some money!

This place just seems to go from one crisis to another. There are some amazing stories; I'll save them for another letter. They keep offering to give me some training but why bother. It would probably just ruin all my natural talents. Anyhow, I have a pretty darn good idea what clients need, and I have excellent contact with them. You don't need a degree in social work for that. In fact, it helps that I'm on their level so to speak, and don't use fancy words. I also use the fact that I'm unpaid to show them I really care.

There are some advantages to volunteer work here. As a volunteer, I set my own hours, and feel pretty much free to do as I please. I always say they can't fire me, whatever I do. And when I have complaints I go right to the top. After all, I'm a citizen, a voter, and a taxpayer.

Staff don't smile at me much or say "thank you," like they ought to. In fact, the only considerate one is that nice Mr. Miller who sometimes drops by to suggest I go home early.

If you're paid for your work, such courtesies aren't a big thing. For me they are. And how about a free parking space (Mr. Miller has one)? Would you believe many staff don't even show up at the annual "Spotlight on Volunteers" Recognition Banquet. Last year, the Major gave a great speech congratulating us on all the money we were saving the City. We had a wonderful gourmet banquet, and believe me, lots of exquisite formal gowns there.

Incidentally, though I don't care, of course, several friends have mentioned their surprise I didn't get the volunteer of the year award at last year's banquet. True enough, I put in the 693 ½ hours last year.

Well, got to write a few more letters.

Ta, Ta

Viola

Viola Stradivarious

Chapter 2: Respecting Staff Concerns

Confidentially, Volunteers Can...

In agencies dealing with sensitive information, keeping confidentiality is a frequent staff worry about volunteers. Do not treat this as if it were a screen for some less valid source of resistance. Instead, treat the issue with all the respect due a plausible concern.

Also, do not go the finger-pointing route: "Nyah, nyah, I've seen you staff people make some horrible slips, too." Maybe so, but this just raises red flags, and does nothing to deal with the overall challenge of confidentiality for all agency personnel, volunteers as well as staff. I would use the "you, too" approach only in extremity, as a response to some staff who insist on telling horror stories about individual volunteers breaching confidentiality.

A common staff misconception is that the need for confidentiality is a rare necessity in only a few occupations. To confront this, ask staff to brainstorm all the occupations in which ability to handle confidential information is necessary or highly desirable. They might be surprised at the length of the list, which numbers over fifty occupations, including: lawyer, accountant, clergy, bartender, financial counselor, stockbroker, beautician, barber, banker, fraternal organization member, doctor, nurse, psychologist, social worker, banker, teacher, credit agency employee, secretary, and on and on. Add here, too, boards of directors made up of volunteers and that probably includes the agency's own board. (So we already have volunteers handling confidential material in this agency!)

Once this list has gotten good and long, suggest that if staff remain worried, we recruit as volunteers only people who are or were in any of these occupations once and/or are in the immediate family of such people. That probably works out to at least a third of all people in most communities. That is, unless you add "friend" and "parent" to the list of "confidential occupations" and then it's close to 100%!

Staff nightmares about volunteer access to sensitive information might also unconsciously assume this means volunteers have potential access to all confidential information in agency files. But this is rarely necessary or desirable. Instead, observe the "principle of minimum information." A volunteer should have access only to that information which is absolutely necessary in her/his work, which is probably only one case record. (This may be an excellent principle for staff, too.)

In defining the extent of minimum feasible information to provide volunteers, one "stopper" may be whether or not it is legal for volunteers to have such information. Conversely, some information considered confidential by staff may actually be, by law, open to public access. In the latter situation, you'll have to decide whether confrontation or quiet acceptance is in the best ultimate interests of clients and the volunteer program. One pointer is to assure everyone that all volunteers will, of course, also be thoroughly oriented, trained, and supervised in regard to confidentiality.

Finally, be aware of this apparent paradox on minimum information for volunteers: be aware of it, but *use* it only judiciously, if at all. A volunteer concentrating one-to-one on a single case will soon know far more about that case than a staff person with a large caseload ever could. So the question may not be how much sensitive information staff are willing to share with volunteers; the question is how much information volunteers are willing to share with staff! Hopefully, the volunteer will trust the staff person with all this sensitive information!

Maybe you'll never be able to persuade some staff people. Then work with the ones who are persuaded. Some may claim they'd like volunteers to work with cases, *without* being entrusted with confidential information. To these, you'll probably have

Building Staff/Volunteer Relations © 2003 Energize, Inc.

Chapter 2: Respecting Staff Concerns

to point out that if you don't trust a volunteer with all the relevant information on a case, you shouldn't trust them with the case.

The "terminal" situation is where no staff believe volunteers should be trusted with confidential material, or else agency policy generally forbids it. In that case, keep trying to change agency policy and meanwhile hope there are significant things volunteers are willing to do which don't require access to confidential information on clients. Shhhhh...

Will They Take My Job Away (Or My Budget)?

This is the hardest fear of all for staff to express openly. It is also the most powerful, usually. And it is the major concern of labor unions. I suggest you meet it head on.

Via hinting or hounding, the message is: recruit more volunteers to replace paid employees. The implication is that paid staff losses can be entirely made up as if by magic; neither quality nor intensity of services will suffer. The disturbing question for all of us is:

> *Will volunteers (inadvertently) make human service budget cuts appear to be more feasible and bearable, thus easier to justify and harder to restore?*

The answer is no, but there is a surface plausibility to the proposition, and much damage is done simply because many people believe it. The following is a reasoned set of reassurances about the role of volunteers vis-a-vis paid staff that can be used by you in countering concerns.

Let's first puncture any lingering prejudice that volunteers and their leaders are the deliberate "natural enemies" of paid employees. As already noted, historically, volunteers pioneered every paid position in human services today. Without exception. And this job creation process continues down to the present. Give volunteers meaningful pioneering work today so it can become the paid position of tomorrow.

About two-thirds of today's volunteers are also working somewhere else for pay and volunteer only in their spare time. Someone in the household will be working for money, or has at one time done so, in 90% or more cases for a volunteer. How absurd then to claim that volunteers don't know what it's like to be working stiffs or are unsympathetic to the problems of wage earners.

A recent Gallup Poll asked people to give reasons why they volunteered. Among eight reasons given, the lowest was "volunteer work helps keep taxes or other costs down." Only 5% of people gave this as among their reasons for volunteering, and none of the other listed reasons were even faintly anti-staff. Indeed, it stands to reason that the vast majority of people who volunteer for your agency do so because they see the importance of what you're doing and would like to strengthen it.

Treated with respect and trust, well oriented and trained, given meaningful work to do, these volunteers can become a powerful, positive constituency for you in the community. They vote. They write letters to the editor. They attend town meetings. They have their own extensive networks. And sometimes they run for office. Why not form a "Friends of ____" group for your agency to facilitate volunteer advocacy on your behalf? Warmly invite all your service volunteers to belong. It is crucial that staff begin to see volunteers more as a constituency and less as some strange species of pseudo-staff.

Building Staff/Volunteer Relations © 2003 Energize, Inc.

Chapter 2: Respecting Staff Concerns

In any event, decently treated volunteers are ordinarily on the side of the agency, not the budget-blasters. But suppose some decision-makers go ahead anyhow because they think paid staff layoffs can be fully substituted for by increased numbers of volunteers. Some very serious questions should be asked of those who would replace paid staff wholesale with volunteers. Here are a few:

- *Is it legal?*

Is this a responsibility that can legally be assumed by volunteers in lieu of paid employees? Even if volunteers can assume full legal responsibility and accountability, can they and the agency be sufficiently safeguarded by insurance and legal immunities incident to the performance of such duties by volunteers?

- *Do you really expect to get enough appropriate volunteers substantially to replace staff slots?*

Assume the average volunteer works about two or three hours a week at any particular job. It would then take about 15 volunteers to replace one full-time paid employee, plus a few more volunteers to coordinate the other 15. Round that to a 20:1 ratio. If you're seriously claiming fully to replace one paid employee in this way, plausibility is shattered by several absurdities:

~ You'd have to be exquisitely fortunate to get twenty volunteers with skills and experience equivalent to the replaced paid staffer. Such jigsaw luck would be too rare to make much difference overall.

~ Coordination, consistency, and continuity of effort would be horrendously difficult.

~ Where would you get twenty volunteers of any kind to substitute for each paid employee? The latest polls tell us that about fifty percent of Americans already volunteer. For the other fifty percent, the competition is increasingly fierce; the estimate is that five to seven times as many organizations are competing for volunteers compared to just a decade ago.

No wonder then, that there's generally a volunteer shortage today; many fine organizations have been steadily losing volunteers or struggling desperately just to stay even. In this situation, it is tragically silly to be asked (usually suddenly) to increase your volunteer workforce twenty-fold, even ten-fold or two-fold. Indeed, a convincing case can be made that replacing all human and government service personnel in a community with volunteers would take more new volunteers than there are available people in that community!

- *Will you supervise and support volunteers adequately?*

Volunteer motivation and effectiveness depend heavily on good supervision and support by agency personnel. Agency accountability for what volunteers do also requires this. But there is a limit to the number of volunteers one paid staff person can adequately supervise (as a rough general rule, 30-40). Once this ceiling is reached, more volunteers require more paid staff to supervise them, or else we risk all the dangers of unsupervised, ineffective, frustrated volunteers. In fact, experience teaches that the number of volunteers and paid staff in an agency often tends to go up or down together. This is just the opposite of the inverse relation envisaged by the replacers: more volunteers as there are fewer staff.

Volunteers, of course, must fill important needs when there are no paid employees to do so. Here we should be careful to distinguish two cases. In the first case, there never were paid employees to perform the service and there are unlikely to be any in the foreseeable future; for example, the rural volunteer fire department. A very different case is where paid employees have been seriously cut back or eliminated; for example, a library branch all of whose staff have been laid off. As in the first case, volunteers will still have to pick up this service (temporarily), if it is to be preserved at all. But here, it should be done under clear and forceful protest, promises to remember come election time, etc.

Where some staff remain, there is, of course, a vital role for volunteer programs in human service agencies. This role is to support, enrich, and multiply the efforts of paid staff, not to replace them. Indeed, the only genuinely healthy growth of volunteer programs works **with** paid staff, not **against** them.

Those who use the volunteer movement as an excuse for deeper cuts in human services are either extraordinarily naive or willfully manipulative. They should be made to say what they really mean: that they are willing to sacrifice quality and intensity of services to needy people, in favor of other priorities they have. They should not be allowed to invoke volunteers as a kind of magic which gets them off that hook. The last thing volunteers should be used for is further disservice to the weak and vulnerable of a nation, and damage to volunteerism itself through the raising of unrealistic expectations.

Is all this a deliberate conspiracy to "use" volunteers in the ugliest sense of that word? Probably not, in most cases. More often, it is a dangerous naivete we have not had sufficient courage to confront. We can begin to do so, by discreet hissing of politicians who praise volunteers primarily for the money they save. Then add some loud cheers for anyone who praises staff-with-volunteers for the multiplier effect in their partnership.

The Selective Success Approach

Let's say you're thinking of introducing volunteers into your agency, or introducing them on a substantially larger scale. And you'd like to minimize immediate and ongoing resistance from staff. Further, let's say you have three staff members to whom volunteers might be assigned:

~ Frank Miller, whom we already know is frankly anti-volunteer, though he tends to deny it. As of now you'd get willing acceptance of volunteers over Frank's dead body.

~ Jenny Silver has perhaps a little ambivalence, but is willing to give it a try once she's taken care of some other current priorities.

~ Linda Gold has plenty of volunteer experience herself, is enthusiastic, knowledgeable about volunteers, and rarin' to go.

Chapter 2: Respecting Staff Concerns

Now, assuming you have a choice, who would you work with to get volunteers productively involved (or more involved) in the agency?

Let us hope you don't have to deal with some compulsively standardized edict which insists that each and every staff member have a minimum of, say, five volunteers within some specified time (usually unrealistically short). This foolish fiat allows you to break your heart trying to persuade the essentially unpersuadable Frank, with little energy left over to capitalize on the truly positive opportunities offered by working with Linda.

Even worse would be to try to prove something by "going after" Frank first. While the broadside approach to all three could be partly successful, a Frank-first masochistic method is sheer suicide (at least for now). Not incidentally, it's terribly unfair to the volunteers who end up entrusted to Frank's tender mercies. Sort of, if you don't like the wind, steer straight for the hurricane.

By contrast, the selective success strategy concentrates first on working with Linda, supporting her in having the finest possible success experience with her first group of volunteers, and being sure she gets lots of deserved praise in the right places. Then, maybe Jenny will edge in a bit. At that point, it's best if Linda takes the lead in talking peer-to-peer with Jenny, rather than you as the "designated volunteer advocate."

Frank? Maybe never, and please realize there might still be a great deal of good in him as a person and a staff member. (Read his speech with this in mind.) On the other hand, maybe someday, somehow, with an expanded and clarified view of volunteers, and with the success examples within his own agency, Frank will have a change of view and change of heart. Even so, with the Franks of this world, the first volunteers you send in might be avowedly a kind of commando beachhead squad, especially strong in being able to work with (and surreptitiously teach) folks like Frank. They must also be particularly sensitive to the fact that they'll be working with Frank as much as with clients.

Another tactic, if you feel surrounded by Franks, is to have yourself, as volunteer coordinator, become the only, or main, staff person supervising volunteers in the agency, and, as such, run a model program. Observing how well it goes may make other staff more inclined to consider volunteers in their work much as the selective success process works in other ways. The limitation on this model program approach is the ceiling on how many volunteers one coordinator can effectively supervise.

But usually there'll be a Linda Gold or two in the agency, and a Jenny Silver behind her. So, go for the Gold (Linda, that is) and then the Silver, and hope Frank isn't out of the race forever.

The selective success approach usually applies to units or divisions within an organization, in much the same way as it applies to individuals. The general principle is identical: move with what's moving, first.

In smaller agencies, the volunteer advocate will usually be aware of degrees of receptivity to volunteers among different individuals or units. The Lindas, Jennys, and Franks aren't so hard to tell apart, once you get to know them. In larger organizations, however, the "Perspectives on Volunteers" checklist on the next page is a useful aid to diagnosis, and in any size organization it can serve as a stimulus to discussion. Offer anonymity to those staff who for any reason want that choice. As with any checklist, feel free to modify wording appropriate to your situation

Building Staff/Volunteer Relations © 2003 Energize, Inc.

Perspectives On Volunteers

A Checklist for Individual Staff

Date: _____
Name (Optional): _____
Role in Organization: _____
Relationship to Volunteer Program: _____

Rate each of the statements below for yourself as a staff person on the following scale:

    0 = Strongly disagree
    1 = Disagree
    2 = In-between
    3 = Agree
    4 = Strongly agree

If you are not working with volunteers, try to answer the questions on a "what if" or speculative bas.

Rating

1. A team of volunteers-plus-staff can do a better job than staff alone. _____

2. The time and effort I invest supervising volunteers is worth whatever additional benefits accrue from their service (it's better than just doing it myself). _____

3. Volunteers do things which are inefficient for me to do and allow better investment of my time elsewhere. _____

4. Volunteer participation enables me to do additional things I wouldn't otherwise be able to do. _____

5. I feel I have enough direction/control of what volunteers do, so that they are accountable. _____

6. I feel sufficient ownership of the volunteer program generally via my policy or operational participation in such program functions as recruiting, screening, design of volunteer jobs, training of volunteers, evaluation, etc. _____

7. Volunteers are well-oriented towards sensitive understanding of my priorities, concerns, and frustrations as a staff person. _____

8. I receive suitable orientation and training in the special skills and sensitivities necessary for effective supervision of volunteers. _____

9. As a staff person, I feel I receive enough recognition for effective work in supervising volunteers. _____

Building Staff/Volunteer Relations

© 2003 Energize,

10. I'm completely comfortable about volunteers' abilities to handle confidentiality or other sensitive work issues. _____

11. I'm confident volunteers can be utilized positively to support our work, rather than as an excuse for cutting our budget. _____

12. Please put in here and rate, any feature not covered above which affects your motivation to work with volunteers. _____

_____

Raw Total _____

Multiply raw total by 2 and give yourself 4 more points for being a good person:

Adjusted Total _____

Your adjusted total can range from 4 to 100 (most positive) for your perspective on volunteers. Now answer this last question:

Overall, I feel that my rating of my motivation to work with/supervise volunteers is: __

Is there something that might be done to address your motivation to work with volunteers in any of the twelve areas for which your self-assessment is relatively low? What suggestions might be helpful to the volunteer program leadership? Use this checklist as a basis for an action plan.

Building Staff/Volunteer Relations

© 2003 Energize, Inc.

Chapter 2: Respecting Staff Concerns

Satisfy Staff First

The Job Factor Process

As we have already discussed, most strategies for opening up participation by volunteers tend to assume that staff are the primary cause of the blockage. "If only staff would respect and trust volunteers more," we say; "if only they weren't so threatened" and "why can't they delegate more?"

The approach here, by contrast, asks certain questions which suggest that staff are not the primary reason for the difficulty. Planners/implementers of volunteer programs are very likely to be implicated, for lack of adopting appropriate strategies. Our candidate for appropriate strategy begins with this question:

> *How can we expect staff to carve out meaningful roles for volunteers when staff doesn't even adequately understand their own role?*

Yes, most employees have a formal job description. But often what a person actively does is far from identical to the job description as written. At the specific, concrete level, what one does daily is more or other than what may have been articulated at the beginning. Not incidentally, the same is true for volunteer job descriptions. They're neat, comforting to our sense of orderliness, and often substantially mythical in detailed practice.

Once we've absorbed the need to go beyond job descriptions to actual descriptions of the job, we're ready to face a seeming paradox: you can't develop clear and meaningful volunteer jobs without first analyzing in detail what staff are doing and how they feel about it. Similarly, to involve members more meaningfully you must first scrutinize very carefully what elected officers or other group leaders are doing.

So, the first step in developing teamwork between volunteers and employees (or officers) is a process which helps staff clarify fuzzy function areas.

The clarifying process must also be comfortable, and that brings up our second main point:

> *Volunteers must be seen by staff as strengthening their capability and control rather than stretching it thinner.*

Volunteers should enhance staff competency rather than challenge it.

As for control, asking staff to work comfortably with volunteers is asking them to forego the two main mechanisms by which we exercise adequate control over employees:

Building Staff/Volunteer Relations

~ We pay them (and can stop doing so).

~ We order them (and can continue to do so).

A third control-threatener is overstretched time. Staff, club leaders, chairpersons and other gatekeepers are typically overworked and under-helped; that's usually why we propose involving volunteers in the first place. We then proceed (often) to lecture staff on how much additional time and effort they should invest in supervising/supporting volunteers. To this approach, I once heard a staff person react thusly: "Hey, I've already got a caseload of 70 clients. And now you seem to be asking me to add a caseload of 25 volunteers. Are you out of your mind?" (Frank Miller, you will recall, felt much the same way.)

I sympathize. We need a delegation process which puts staff in the driver's seat insofar as possible and, indeed, can be seen by them as enhancing their control of events and challenges. This is not accomplished by coming in, kicking the desk, and saying to staff: "Wow, I've got this great volunteer; wouldn't you like to meet her?" or "How about my getting you a volunteer tutor or two?"

It is not even accomplished by asking staff to submit volunteer job descriptions. As I said, many staff need a better, more specific understanding of their own jobs before they can intelligently decide how volunteers can best help them. So, we err in telling staff to look at volunteers when they should be looking first at themselves.

Helping Staff Look at Their Own Work First

We need to give staff a specific, practical process for looking at themselves. The process proposed here is called "Job Factoring." It is in a direct line of descent from a method called "Need Overlap Analysis in Helping" (NOAH) first developed about twenty-five years ago and widely applied in field practice since then. The Job Factor is an advanced version of this approach, sometimes called NOAH-III. Here are some general guidelines for facilitating the Job Factoring process:

1. Clearly explain step-by-step procedures, with examples (as described in the next section).

2. Explanations can be on an individual or group basis, but each staff/gatekeeper does her/his work as an individual.

3. Give people plenty of time to complete the process, at least overnight and preferably a few days, over which they can come back to it periodically, and enlarge or modify their Job Factor.

4. Assure staff that supervisors will not be looking over their shoulder. Sharing of their Job Factor, in whole or in part, is on an entirely voluntary basis.

5. In some situations, you might also want to note that completion of the process does not commit a person to accepting volunteer or other help with their job. Indeed, Job Factors are great aids to insight about one's work, even if they don't lead to suggestions on how volunteers might help.

Here is the step-by-step process.

Step 1: Ask the person to make an *Activity List* (to be called the "A List"):

Think of your last few days (or week) at work and list, fairly specifically, all the things you did work-wise during that time.

Note that it's usually difficult to remember all one's tasks and activities at one time. Some people like to be sure of a complete list by keeping a log of their activities for a few days. A complete Activity List might well contain 30 or 40 distinct activities, possibly even more. Figures 1, 2 and 3 on the following pages are examples of this.

Step 2: Now mark your Activity List as follows:

~ "X" marked after an activity means that you believe you would be more effective and satisfied as a worker if you could get someone else to take this off your hands. (These are called "spin-off" or "up-for-grabs" tasks.)

~ "T" marked by an activity means you'd be more effective and satisfied if you could team it, do it with someone else. Clearly, that's not the same as a spin-off. You do want to continue doing the task and keep a hand in policy concerning it; you just want some company with it, a partner or teammate.

~ A circle around a task means you feel this is a "keeper," pretty much the core or center of what you do, an "essential." You definitely want to keep doing this by yourself. You might easily have four or five keepers.

~ None of the above. Put a question mark (?) by these activities. It's okay to give yourself more time to decide on some things.

Step 3: Now, in another, second column, make your DREAM LIST (the "D List").

These are things you would love to do or see happen for the benefit of the organization and the people it serves. However, these things are not being done now, either because you (or others) don't have the time, don't have the resources, or have neither time nor resources. Take your time pondering this list, too, and try to come up with two to five "good dreams."

Step 4: Now prepare a QUEST LIST (or any name that suits you better).

This "Q List" describes fairly specific things you'd like to learn more about, and/or areas in which you'd like to learn and grow.

Chapter 3: Satisfy Staff First

Activities The "A" List	Dreams The "D" List	Quests or Yearns-to-Learn The "Q" List	Pleasant Surprises The P.S. List
Answer Correspondence ? Prepare newspaper article T (Attend staff meetings) Keep statistics X Answer routine phone X inquiries Work on annual report T Take photos for slide X show (Interview volunteers) (Work on policy for volunteers) Lay out fall recruiting ? campaign Plan next orientation for ? volunteers Select recognition items T Supervise volunteers in X office Arrange potluck supper X	Develop fund to reimburse volunteer expenses Have regular staff orientation to volunteers Get good film(s) on volunteers Be able to go on at least one out of state training per year	Conflict management Financial planning Public Speaking Fund-raising techniques	

Figure 1: Sample Job Factor for a Coordinator of Volunteers
(If we don't delegate, who will?)

Chapter 3: Satisfy Staff First

Activities The "A" List	Dreams The "D" List	Quests or Yearns-to-Learn The "Q" List	Pleasant Surprises The P.S. List
(Organize agendas for board meeting)	That we can publish proceedngs of this year's conference	Time management	
(Preside at board meetings)		More on how to delegate effectively	
Write future grants X	Raise enough money to hire a part-time staff person	Public speaking skills	
(Oversee planning for this year's conference)			
Plan future conferences X	That at least 20% of our members will be actively involved on committees		
(Approve all expenditures)			
Sign checks T			
Encourage networking ? among members			
Do newsletter T			
Meet "visiting dignitaries" ?			
Upgrade membership list T			
(Represent us at meetings of other groups)			
Seek talent to involve ? among members			

Figure 2: Sample Job Factor for a President of an All-Volunteer Educational Group *(Adapted, in some respects. Thus, original is much longer with 31 items on the "A" List.)*

Chapter 3: Satisfy Staff First

Activities The "A" List	Dreams The "D" List	Quests or Yearns-to-Learn The "Q" List	Pleasant Surprises The P.S. List
Do pre-sentence investigation T Wait in court til case called X (Attend staff meetings) Check on referrals to other agencies ? (Counsel with intensive cases) Counsel families of clients ? Help get jobs for clients T Answer routine info requests (by phone) X Give talks to schools T Escort "violent" offenders ? to jail Visit jailed probationers ? Compile stats for monthly reports T (Represent department at human services coalition) Transport clients to medical or psychological attention X	Establish revolving loan fund for worthy probationers Get part-time admin. asst. so I have more time for counseling Get accurate, comprehensive list of community resourses Better working relations with jail administration & staff	Learn stress management Learn more about career counseling Learn to control temper Become a better problem-solver	

Figure 3: Sample Job Factor for a Probation Officer

Chapter 3: Satisfy Staff First

Step 5: Finally, set up a fourth column with the heading PLEASANT SURPRISES (the "P.S. Column").

Leave this column blank for now but (we hope) not forever. All this column indicates is that you are flexible enough to make room for involving unanticipated time and talent which might be offered you or the organization, provided it shows prospects of benefit to all concerned.

Throughout, keep reminding people to be as specific and concrete as possible in all their listings. Figures 1, 2, and 3 on the following pages are adapted examples of real-life Job Factors.

From the Job Factor to Volunteer Jobs

The Job Factor process facilitates precise delegation from staff to volunteers in a way which gives staff genuine ownership of the volunteer program. Here's what we have to work from:

~ Overall patterns in the job factor.

~ The Activity List ("A List") with unmarked items, spin-offs/up-for-grabs items (Xs), Ts for teaming with another, and circled items essential to the job.

~ The Dream List ("D List")

~ The Quest List ("Q List")

~ Pleasant Surprises ("P.S. List")

Overall Pattern

Willingness and ability to delegate to volunteers tend to increase when the Job Factors include a healthy number of spinoffs, teams, dreams, and quests because these define the work which is potentially delegatable to volunteers. It is also important that relatively few of the spin-offs, teams, dreams and quests are excluded out of hand by an "authority check," e.g., violate union contract; are illegal for volunteers to do; are against organizational policy or encountering strong staff feelings that this job should be paid for. It is also good if a reasonable proportion of remaining possibilities go beyond routine tasks to more meaningful, challenging work—which usually means there are Quests and Dreams along with the often drudge spin-offs.

Potential for delegation to volunteers is weaker if the above conditions are not met. Thus, some staff seem uneasy about "admitting" that they have any spin-offs, apparently for fear it will show they aren't really needed. Watch for very short D and Q lists; the staff/gatekeeper who is afraid to dream and/or unwilling to concede that s/he has anything to learn. Watch, too, for staff who are seriously put off by the openness of the concept of the Pleasant Surprise column. My strong hunch is that volunteers first of all tend to be more for those willing to concede they need help (all listings). After that, volunteers are more for dreamers, questers, the flexible and creative among staff/gatekeepers.

Building Staff/Volunteer Relations © 2003 Energize, Inc.

In any case, use the overall Job Factor pattern in the above ways to identify an individual staff person's receptivity to volunteer help. If that receptivity seems low, remember s/he may still be a fine staff person in other respects, then go to more receptive staff first in advocating and placing volunteers. (See earlier discussion in Chapter 2.)

The Activity List

Spin-offs (X's) aren't always or necessarily drudge items, especially in the perception of some volunteers. But if spin-offs are all staff seem willing to offer volunteers—no teams, dreams, or other meaningful responsibilities—we may have a problem here. Either the program is new and needs to learn to trust volunteers more (give it some time to do that) and/or the staff person suffers from stale stereotypes as to what volunteers are capable of doing.

T's offer great potential for encouraging staff to move on to "higher" things in delegation to volunteers. In the first place, staff can still keep their hand in on a team task; they don't have to let go and "give it up" entirely. At the same time, team tasks often represent somewhat more responsible volunteer work than spin-offs do.

When you see circled, essential items, STAY AWAY! For now at least. I shudder to think how much resistance to volunteer programs is due to going for staff's Job Factor jugular first; that is, their keepers. All too typically, this is done without specifically consulting staff or even giving them an opportunity to realize that this is the core of what they do. At any one point in a program there will usually be plenty of other things volunteers can do, many of them quite meaningful.

Later, after trust builds, you might begin gently to suggest that some keepers could be at least partly "upgraded" to teams or even spin-offs. Thus, "interview volunteers," a keeper for the coordinator in Figure 1, could evolve to a point where a volunteer first "job shadows" the coordinator in such interviews, then teams on a few more, and perhaps later does take a few of them by her/himself (spin-off).

Look for question-marked items, such as "meeting visiting dignitaries" in Figure 2. Lack of any X, T or circle markings might simply mean the staff person is undecided on this and/or needs more information. Don't press. In fact, be very clear that it's okay to have activity listings "question-marked" for a time. On the other hand, after a while it might gently be suggested that subdividing such items could clarify their status.

Thus, in Figure 1, "plan next orientation for volunteers" could break out into sub-tasks such as:

~ Review feedback from last year's volunteer orientation

~ Set agenda

~ Select and invite trainers

~ Search out appropriate films and other training aids

This kind of breakout might more easily suggest delegation possibilities.

The Dream List

The demonstration here is that volunteers can help us do things we desperately want to do, but never could accomplish without their help. That's a powerful motivator for many frustrated staff. Un-frustrating their pursuit of dreams is a great way to prevent staff burnout. And over and over again, volunteers have demonstrated they can help make dreams come true for an organization. Indeed, this was the historical role of volunteers: putting flesh on dreams that never would have happened otherwise; creating and justifying new services and facilities before society was prepared to pay for them.

But don't let volunteers take dreams away from staff. That's as bad as encroaching on staff "keepers." Generally, make the advancement of dreams a team enterprise between staff and volunteers. Or enable staff to have more time to achieve their dreams because of volunteers helping them with their activity list (spin-offs and teams).

The Quest List

As indicated earlier, the kind of staff/gatekeeper who can't think of anything much s/he needs to learn is probably not a good bet to delegate much meaningful work to volunteers. Where you do find at least a few "yearn-to-learns," there is a tremendous opportunity to puncture restrictive staff stereotypes on the level of work volunteers can handle.

In one program where a pattern in staff quests suggested the need for a workshop on creative problem-solving, the coordinator brought in a professional trainer to do the workshop—as a volunteer. That fact was not lost on staff.

Pleasant Surprises

This blank column is to remind us that we can make meaningful volunteer job placements not only by "selling" staff-designed work to volunteers (the usual way), but also in the other direction: by marketing volunteer talents to staff. For example, suppose a person who likes to play piano and is good at it, walks in to a nursing home. The creative coordinator might respond by launching a music hour weekly. Some situations may require more stretching. An optometrist offered his services to a Juvenile Probation Department. Well, Juvenile Probation Departments aren't supposed to be in the eye-testing business. But this one had a creative judge who built a program around this person's offering. Result: about half the kids coming through the court proved to have significant visual problems which had slipped through more superficial school screening. All this, of course, had profound significance for alternative understanding of why some of these kids had trouble reading and with school generally.

To prime the pump for pleasant surprises, present staff with a composite list of "glad gifts" offered by volunteers or potential volunteers. These are fairly specific things the volunteers like to do and can do pretty well. Ten volunteers might have 250 to 300 of these glad gifts, in a wondrous range and variety. Only a truly stunted imagination could fail to be tempted by this great richness of offering and staff might begin to fill the pleasant surprise column with the seeds of productive programs. (There's more on glad gifts in the next chapter.)

Chapter 3: Satisfy Staff First

Processing for Matches

Organizations differ; no two sets of conditions are the same. Use your own best judgment on how to move toward matches between staff needs and volunteer offerings. These are just a few suggestions.

Caution staff/gatekeepers against overexpectation. If 15 to 20% of their work assistance needs (X + T + D + Q) can be helped by volunteer offerings, that's great (and is, in fact, a rough average based on field usage of this process). But too often, staff go in one fell swoop from expecting nothing of volunteers to expecting everything. So please be sure gatekeepers don't anticipate instant, comprehensive satisfaction.

A former colleague says she sometimes feels staff thinks she has a huge freezer well stocked with a wide selection of quick-frozen volunteers. She can instantly retrieve precisely the right size and shape volunteers, put them in her people-sized microwave for a minute and presto! ...'Tain't so.

The raw staff request list of spin-offs, teams, dreams, and quests can easily reach 25 or more for a single gatekeeper, and hundreds when combined over even a relatively small staff. This is so even when staff clearly understand that their work assistance needs are to be shared only voluntarily at their own discretion.

Especially in agency settings, the following criteria should usually be applied to narrow down the raw list of staff/gatekeeper work assistance needs. As indicated previously, the criteria for elimination are:

The Authority Check:
~ it violates union contract for volunteers to perform this task;

~ it's against organizational policies;

~ legally, this responsibility must remain with a paid employee, including paid employees with specific credentials and/or training; and

~ for some reason, staff feel strongly that people should be paid to do this (and maybe some volunteers feel the same way).

After applying these criteria, you may find that the total work assistance request list has been cut by 20 to 50%. Keep trying to change the situation if you think a task is something volunteers ought to be able to do. Pending such change, however, work within the framework as you find it. There will still almost always be lots of meaningful things volunteers might do among many remaining spin-offs, teams, dreams and quests.

The Consensus Check:
Spin-offs, Teams, Quests and Dreams with which staff tend to agree they need help are most likely to engender an overall agency atmosphere of support for volunteer involvement. Nevertheless, don't completely ignore the Dream, Quest, Team or Spin-off only one person has. The lonely dream is sometimes the most creative one. So arrange to bring it up again next year, perhaps.

The Consumer Check:
If at all possible, have a committee of consumers/clients/patients review the winnowed-down staff work assistance needs list with two issues in mind: "is

Building Staff/Volunteer Relations © 2003 Energize, Inc.

Chapter 3: Satisfy Staff First

this really a priority of ours?" and "even if it's a priority, would we rather try to do it ourselves?" Thus, for the staff dream of a good video on neighborhood problems, consumers might suggest as higher priority a good video on things neighbors are doing to attack those problems—and they might want to film it themselves!

The still substantial staff need list remaining (X+ T + D + Q) can be matched with volunteer offerings in a number of ways. But first we have to do everything possible to be sure we have a good grip on all that volunteers are willing to offer and, equally important, that they are *not* willing to offer. The recommended method for doing this is to generate a "Window of Work" with each volunteer or potential volunteer. We'll describe this in the next chapter. Essentially this is the fullest possible listing of the person's "glad gifts" (to be described), quests (the same as in the staff Job Factor) and no-no's/aversions/taboos.

Chapter 3: Satisfy Staff First

4 Satisfying Work for Volunteers

The Window of Work Process

Having given staff the opportunity to analyze and dream about their own jobs, and to consider the ways they might be supported by volunteers, we can now turn to the question of how best to design work for volunteers.

Philosophy, First

How do we get people to work? When you think of it, there are only three ways:

We give them *dollars,*
We give them *orders,* or
We give them *reasons.*

Pay, pressure, or persuasion—some mix of these three is what prompts most people to work. The rare and exquisite handicap for volunteer leadership is that we have only the last one. This sometimes makes motivating volunteers seem like trying to run a four-minute mile under water.

So, scratch money and mandate as main incentives, and look hard at persuasion. Here, many volunteer leaders think first of rewards outside the work itself: pins, buttons, badges, certificates, gold watches, Mickey Mouse watches, etc. This can be nice but it's only the icing on the cake; the real substance of volunteer motivation is the work we offer people, the job itself. This is an intrinsic motivation.

We know this first of all from ancient wisdom, thus: "The wise leader knows that the reward for doing the work arises naturally out of the work." Current evidence further confirms this. Gallup Polls have identified the main reasons Americans give for volunteering. Of eight reasons given with significant frequency, the top three were:

~ Like doing something useful, helping others

~ Am interested in the activity

~ Enjoy doing the work, feeling needed

Make no mistake about it, the work itself is by far the most powerful motivator of volunteers. That is the first surprise for some who assume that other, extrinsic incentives, are the key.

The second surprise is that the work-motivation a person brings to us is almost always sufficient to fill the needs of our organization. We don't have to reach down inside people and adjust their drive mechanisms. Actually, "motivate" as a verb is somewhat disrespectful of the kinds of quality people who come to us as volunteers. To repeat, the notion that appropriate volunteer placement needs first to manipulate a person's motivation is usually fallacious and always arrogant. Instead, we can accept the motivation people bring with them; almost always this is good enough, in the sense that somewhere there is work we need that this motivation will power.

To summarize our two main assumptions at this point, hoping that what follows will persuade you of them:

~ The work itself is the main motivator of volunteers.

~ In adult human beings we don't create motivation; we identify it, accept it, and then connect it creatively to organizational and community needs.

Motivational Markers

The "Window of Work" process is based on these two assumptions. The procedure identifies the work which most motivates a volunteer and at the same time is useful to the host organization. The process is a simple, effective tool for use in connection with interviewing, placing, and matching volunteers. It provides a profile of existing motivation for work which is:

~ specific;

~ anchored in visible behavior;

~ comprehensive; and yet

~ practical, in terms of realistically available time for interviewing and placing volunteers.

Contrast this with current approaches to volunteer motivation. These tend to be pitched at a somewhat abstract general level. Let's say we determine that a person is high on achievement motivation. This is a good start, but we still need to know exactly what this person likes most to achieve. Thus, I am high on achievement motivation. But the person who would place me appropriately as a volunteer still needs to know specifically what I most want to and can achieve; for example, excellence in logical analysis, written communication, etc. At least by process of elimination, it is equally important to know what I am not interested in or capable of achieving, e.g., fix-it skills, mathematics, etc. Finally, the placement person must also be able to discriminate clearly between my present capabilities and things I only hope to get good at in the future.

Chapter 4: Satisfying Work for Volunteers

The same points apply to other generalized descriptions of volunteer motivation. Thus, to say a person has a high affiliation drive does not tell us specifically what kinds of people this person most prefers to associate with, and least prefers.

The Window of Work process assumes that much can be made of people accepted as they are. The process is respectful of people in another way, too. Once the relatively straightforward procedures are briefly explained and illustrated, people can largely proceed by themselves. That is, via the Window, we can unravel relevant motivation for volunteering without deep-probing or subtly psyching people. We need just ask them, and trust them to tell us what we need to know about their work-relevant motivations.

But we must ask about the right things in the right way. The key here is concentration on three kinds of motivational markers, defined below, with examples immediately following the explanations.

"Glad Gifts"

A Glad Gift is something fairly specific a person likes to do, can do pretty well, and which might be of use to other people. This is what a person is pre-motivated to do, has competence-plus-preference for. Clearly, glad gifts are basic building blocks in designing volunteer jobs.

"Quests"

A Quest or "Yearn-to-Learn" is something fairly specific a person would like to learn, an area in which a person wants to improve. Having such space to breathe and grow built into a volunteer job is a great way to prevent burnout and assure retention of volunteers.

The Quest-of-all-quests, of course, is someone caring enough to help you learn and grow. In catering to quests, the long-term payoff for the organization is freshened motivation and deeper loyalty on the part of the volunteer. The short-term trade-offs are: (a) "loss" of some current volunteer contribution (since by definition a volunteer can't fully perform a quest now) and; (b) the need for an organization to invest time or effort helping the volunteer learn. This means you don't teach people to swim by throwing them in the pool and walking away. All too similarly, in response to my quest for learning to speak Spanish, one organization told me: "We'll put you with Spanish-speaking people." So? Am I supposed to learn Spanish by osmosis, or (better) will at least one of the Spanish-speaking people be asked specifically to help me learn?

"No-No's"

A "no-no", "don't ask," or "taboo" is just what it says. Too many volunteers are too nice to say no when asked to do the detestable, too nice to detail their aversions in the first place. And maybe you're too upbeat to ask. But *do* ask. If you don't, tragic scenes like this ensue: The quiet, seemingly unhappy woman who had been taking notes at the chair's request, later listed as her top aversion—guess what?—taking notes at meetings.

About the second or third time a person is saddled with a no-no, absent special explanation or psychological compensation, you've probably lost them. No matter if the gaffe is inadvertent. Stepping on a person's no-no's, unintentionally or not, probably accounts for most of the otherwise mysterious volunteer burnouts we never seem to understand.

Building Staff/Volunteer Relations © 2003 Energize, Inc.

Chapter 4: Satisfying Work for Volunteers

The irony is, once we know a volunteer's no-no's, it is usually easy to avoid them. You can at least ease the pain by being clear you're asking something rare and special, and have no recourse but to do so.

"Wise Whys"

There is also one other major motivational component, which has something to do with passion and bedrock values, basic life goals and dreams that never die. So far as I know, it can't be fully handled in anything like a formula fashion, though it's no less important for that reason. It has much to do with the fact that while writing is a glad gift of mine, I'd never do it for the Ku Klux Klan and I would do it for, say, a Women's Resource Center. Possibly, we could begin to get close to this value base by requesting completion of a sentence such as: "I think the world would be a better place if _____ ." Personal purpose must not be forgotten.

A person's value base is by no means always easily accessible on the surface. Indications you're getting close include:

~ You start getting "emotional"

~ You stop compromising, "negotiating"

~ Theme(s) emerges through all the volunteer and most meaningful paid work you've done throughout your life

My somewhat abstract grappling with this "fourth factor" was providentially interrupted by a communication from Kitty Gray Carlsen with the Cooperative Extension Service in Washington State. Apparently sensing a similar kind of incompleteness with just the three motivational markers, she "...decided to add a section for volunteers to indicate why they chose to become involved in the organization. I have found that this helps volunteers clarify expectations of involvement and helps us to understand subsequent behaviors!" She calls these "Wise Whys" and thereby comes up with a format which has the additional advantage of looking like a window, as shown on the following page. The instructions for using the Window are:

Window 1:
In the first pane of this window under "Wise Whys," write down why you decided to become a volunteer for this organization.

Window 2:
Under "Glad Gifts," list any talents, skills, interest, hobbies, etc., you do well and that you enjoy doing. If you do it and like it, list it!

Window 3:
The third pane is for listing your "Quests": those things you yearn to learn more about, or skills you would like to develop.

Window 4:
In the fourth pane list what you don't like or what you never want to be asked to do. We call these "Taboos" or "No-no's"

Chapter 4: Satisfying Work for Volunteers

Wise Whys	Glad Gifts
Quests	Taboos

Volunteer Window of Work

Instructions	
Window 1: In the first pane of this window, under "Wise Whys," write down why you decided to become a volunteer for this organization.	*Window 2:* Under "Glad Gifts" list any talents, skills, interests, hobbies, etc. you do well and that you enjoy doing. If you do it and like it, list it!
Window 3: The third pane is for listing your "Quests": those things you yearn to learn more about, or skills you would like to develop.	*Window 4:* In the fourth pane, list what you don't like or what you never want to be asked to do. We call those "Taboos" or "No-no's."

As you can see, I have repeated these instructions on the previous page so that you can duplicate the full page for actual use.

Building Staff/Volunteer Relations © 2003 Energize, Inc.

Chapter 4: Satisfying Work for Volunteers

I do like the four-pane approach, though separate consideration of Wise Whys might not always be necessary. Basic values sometimes come through quite clearly in themes running through Glad Gifts, Quests and No-No's. See especially Caitlin's Window of Work in Figure 3, following on page 47.

Window Shopping

It's time now to move from talking about windows to concrete examples from real life. Three of these are presented in Figures 1, 2, and 3 on the following pages.

Two points occur immediately on looking through these three windows. First, sometimes a phrase or two describing the motivational marker is far from a complete description; for example "collecting humor." Rather than ask the person to write a book on each, which might cut off the flow, use the phrase as a launching point for productive elaboration and perhaps negotiation.

Secondly, never assume out of hand that a glad gift is "useless," however self-oriented it may seem to be. My glad gift of "watching sunsets," for example, once elicited this response: "I work with the blind and invite you to describe sunsets to interested blind people."

In any case, the preceding are fairly typical windows: somewhere around 15 to 20 glad gifts and about half that number of quests and no-no's. The numbers, proportions, and level of concreteness vary widely, of course, and that is perfectly natural. Only extreme patterns need trigger caution; say 50 no-no's and no glad gifts! Or vice versa.

The window imagery comes from an early use of the method with a paid staff person, as it happens. He completed the listings, then said he wished the boss could see them before she delegated or dumped more jobs on him. "I'm sure she'd be more sensitive in work assignments if she had this kind of information in clear, concise form. Know what?" he said, "I think I'm going to put this on my office bulletin board!"

The window format is helpful in presenting personal profiles, though some prefer simply to list the three motivational components, without the window imagery. Nor is there anything sacred about the names "Glad Gift," "Quest," and "No-No." I will however, haunt anyone who substitutes "skill" for "glad gift"! Teaching tennis is a *skill* of mine in the sense that I'm pretty competent at it. I worked my way through college in part by teaching kids to play tennis—and ended up hating kids and tennis. I've more or less recovered on kids, but tennis is still one of my no-no's. Though still a skill. If you somehow persuaded or pressured me to ply this skill you'd probably end up sorry. I certainly would, and so would the kids. So, remember, it's supposed to be a *glad* gift: *preference* along with competence.

Equally beware a preference unaccompanied by competence—the gladness that is *not* a gift. If someone who truly loves archery asks you to stand there with an apple on your head, check first that s/he's also *good* at it.

Chapter 4: Satisfying Work for Volunteers

Glad Gifts	Quests	No-No's

• *Plan meals*
• *Cook/Bake (almost anything)*
• *Informal speaking to groups*
• *Golf*
• *Drive a car*
• *Swim*
• *Gardening-herbs, veggies, and flowers*
• *Hike*
• *Edit, write short articles*
• *Long-term relationships*
• *Play piano*
• *Crossword Puzzles*
• *Teach conflict management*
• *Select, accessorize, harmonize colors in clothing*
• *Dance (waltz, 2-step, polka, free style)*
• *Sew simple garments*
• *Crochet*
• *Manage money*
	• *Write longer articles, a book*
	• *Explore literature, poetry*
	• *Learn to speak French*
	• *Learn to play tennis*
	• *Improve cross-country skiing*
	• *Photography skills*
	• *Improve:*
	    piano skills
	    organ skills
	    ability to judge wine
	    golf
	• *Organize photographs*
	• *Square dance*
	• *Knit*
	• *Identify song birds*
	• *Identify wild flowers*
	• *Improve counseling skills (maybe a master's degree)*
	• *Use a computer*
	• *Understand complicated financial statements*
	• *Improve appreciation and knowledge of symphony, drama, art*
		• *Bowling*
		• *Smoking*
		• *Downhill skiing*
		• *Parachute jumping*
		• *Mountain climbing*
		• *House cleaning*
		• *Bingo*
		• *Fundamental religion*
		• *Smoky rooms*
		• *Weak coffee*
		• *Being controlled or manipulated*
		• *Flagrantly bad grammar or spelling*
		• *Dishonesty*

Figure 1. Barbara Stan's Window of Work (not her real name)

Chapter 4: Satisfying Work for Volunteers

Glad Gifts	Quests	No-No's
• Wash dishes • Draw conclusions from statistical tables • Write (several kinds) • Teach canoeing • Talk about solar power • Vegetable gardening • Help people learn • Walk-hike • Dancing (most kinds) • Cataloguing, classifying books and articles • Compiling survey statistics • Collecting humor • Watching sunsets	• Speak Spanish • More about meditation* • Stir fry cookery • Managing money • Make easy talk with strangers • Play hackey-sack • Make a spontaneous speech • History of Southwest U.S.	• Take meeting notes • Stand in line • Red tape • Teach tennis • Smoky rooms • Asking face-to-face for money, donation • Media commercials • Being late • Other people being late • Being let down by people I must depend on • Working outside when it's colder than 20° F • Talk on telephone

Figure 2. Ivan Scheier's Window of Work *(his real name)*

*Note to reader: Questing doesn't necessarily mean you're totally ignorant in an area. I've meditated for seven years and have taken some formal instruction but that's only whetted my appetite to learn more.

Chapter 4: Satisfying Work for Volunteers

Glad Gifts	Quests	No-No's

• Writing
• Networking people with similar interests
• Introducing people to gourmet vegetarian meals
• Laughing
• Exploring/sharing women's creativity
• Hiking, back-packing
• Jumping in cold mountain streams
• Analyzing political process
• Reading: poetry, philosophy, psychology
• Training:
   group process
   networking
   resource-sharing
   organizational development
• Creative fund-raising
• Playing with cats
• Taking walks around small-ish cities
• Discovering ambiance of a place
• Enjoying silence
• Advocating feminist issues/ "feminizing" society
• Talking about healthy living: food, exercise, self-acceptance
• Growing flowers
	• Facilitate women's creativity groups
	• Publish my writing
	• Live in a rural environment
	• Grow a large garden of vegetables and flowers
	• Find a loving, long-term relationship with a man
	• Learn more about:
	   Being an effective social-change agent
	   Silence and patience
	   Acceptance of people
	   Providing a living space for people in need
	   Self-sufficient living models
	   Multi-media arts projects
		• Rigidity/sloppiness of thought
		• An "end justifies the means" mentality
		• Desire to dominate the eco-system
		• Cruelty to animals
		• Talking for the sake of talking
		• Denial of possibility
		• Crowds
		• Cocktail parties
		• The color orange
		• Polyester pants

Figure 3. Caitlin Downing's Window of Work (not her real name)

Building Staff/Volunteer Relations © 2003 Energize, Inc.

Building Windows

How do we get Windows of Work from volunteers or potential volunteers? Whichever method is used, it helps that the procedure is relatively straightforward and interesting. (At the very least, an open window will be relatively paneless.) In fact, a happy side effect of the process is how important and valued it makes volunteers feel. "Hey, they're not only interested in what I can do for them; they actually want to know what I like to do and even more amazing, what I'd like to learn, and what I don't want to do."

Early on, I suggest you describe the purpose of the window process; for example, "to find volunteer work that fits your motivation as well as our needs." Then show a few sample windows, your own perhaps, or other volunteers' (with permission), and/or the examples just presented here.

It's good to do this face-to-face. To save time, it can be a small group situation. After the explanation and examples, you must usually give people a fair amount of time to complete and polish their windows; a couple of hours at a minimum, even better if it can be overnight or more. Here are some suggestions for making listings as complete as possible:

1. Take your time, take a break from the task and come back to it fresh.

2. Draw from your life at large, not just one part of your life, such as work or home.

3. Go back and forth between the columns. Don't feel you have to get all the Glad Gifts down before you go on to the Quests, etc.

4. Talk through your listings with someone else, and ask for their comments and questions. This should stimulate further free association.

5. Have people who know you well list what they think should be in your window. (You might do the same for them.) They might pick up some things you forgot to list because you do them so frequently and thus, automatically. Or No-No's you tend to repress.

6. When, finally, you seem to be running dry, focus on a series of specific situations, such as "work," "at home," "recreation," and see if that turns up a few more listings to put in your window.

Variations on the Window Format

The Haltom City, Texas Volunteer Program incorporates the window in their volunteer registration form, as shown in Figure 4 on the next page. Another variation in window format, especially adapted to religiously-oriented volunteer programs, was developed by Mary Jo Waters, National Director of LOVE For Children/World Vision. It appears as Figure 5 on page 50.

Another approach would be to mail the window to people well beforehand, with an explanation and examples, and then ask them to bring the draft of their window to the interview.

Chapter 4: Satisfying Work for Volunteers

"Work Window"

Please give some thought to completing the "Work Window" as it will be a primary indicator in helping us locate a special place for you.

In the first pane of the window, under "Special Talents..." list any talents, skills, hobbies, activities, etc. you do well and that you enjoy doing. This could be things such as typing, talking to people, organizing people or projects, writing, working with children, walking dogs, reading, painting, cooking, studying history, operating computers, whatever. Don't hesitate to list it; it might surprise you how your talents could be utilized.

The second pane is to list areas of interest you might not presently have the skills to perform, but which you might enjoy learning about. This could include things such as word processing, Texas history, police communications, city government, landscaping, cable television.

In the third pane, tell us if there is anything you really don't want to do. You might be especially shy and don't want to meet the public, or you may have worked as a secretary and maybe you would rather avoid typing or filing on a volunteer basis. If so, tell us.

By providing this type of information, we hope to tailor your volunteer position just for you. If we can accomplish an enjoyable work environment for you, we accomplish a rewarding and beneficial volunteer experience for both you and the city.

"Work Window"
(Please try to list at least four or five things In each column)

Special skills, talents or interests you like to use	Areas you would like to learn more about	No!

Figure 4
Thanks to Haltom City, Texas Volunteer Program

Overarching belief:
that caring Christian volunteers can change their communities for the better...one life at a time.

Setting...the place(s) you would prefer to work:

-at home
-in an office
-at a WIC/HS site
-at the home of my client
-at a church/public place
-other?_____

Glad Gifts...any talents, skills, interests, and hobbies that you do well and you would enjoy sharing:

-_____
-_____
-_____
-_____
-_____

Relationships... With whom would you prefer to work?

-alone
-in a group
-with one helpee:
-a child
-a mother
-other_____

Quests...those things you would like to learn more about or skills you might like to develop

-_____
-_____
-_____
-_____
-_____

Time Available...or preferred work schedule:

-occasional service
-regular schedule
-1X per week (1-3 hrs.)
-2X per month (1-3 hrs.)
-1X per month (1-3 hrs.)
-other:_____

No! please don't ask:

-_____
-_____
-_____
-_____
-_____
-_____

Volunteer Window of Work

Name of Volunteer: _____
Address: _____
_____
Phone: _____

Figure 5:
Thanks to Mary Jo Waters, National Director of LOVE For Children/World Vision.

Chapter 4: Satisfying Work for Volunteers

Glad gifts, quests and no-no's can also be incorporated as a natural part of the flow in a volunteer interview. This can be one-to-one or in a group situation in which the window process is described and exemplified. Then we all begin building our windows, helping each other do so.

The window process tends to avoid the deep probe proclivities of some other volunteer interview approaches. As further protection of privacy, volunteers should be assured they need not list anything they consider too personal. There will still be plenty of publicly shareable material to build on. A few people may still balk at sharing their window with any stranger. I suggest you ask such people to prepare their window, keep it to themselves, and use it to build their own volunteer job proposals, in relation to the needs of the organization.

There's No Such Thing as a Concrete Window

Each prospective volunteer should have a window of course, but I also suggest the window be regularly re-done for current volunteers, every six months or so. This will first of all demonstrate the program's continuing interest in volunteers as individuals.

It also provides a solid basis for checking the appropriateness of present volunteer assignments, and gives direction to reassignment, or at least rethinking of a volunteer job. Thus, if my desire to learn Spanish has now been taken care of, maybe we need to look at my quest-list for further learning opportunities. In this way, the window of work is as important for preventing volunteer burnout as it is for good placement in the first place. This is because job conditions change, and so does a person's window of work.

The latter point is worth a little elaboration. An individual's window is not cast in concrete; ordinarily, it is far more flexible than glass. In the first place, you are always being reminded of things to add to your window. So, keep it open. There is also a clear pattern of clockwise flow around a window, over longer timespans. Thus, following the window format, a glad gift can sometimes become a no-no through overuse and/or unpleasant associations:

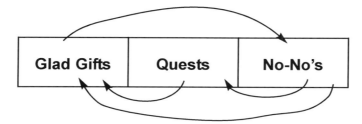

Remember my experience teaching tennis. People don't burn out; functions do. Also, a no-no can become a quest when instruction is a cure for fear or reluctance, and you end up liking it. Say you hate public speaking, are persuaded to take training in it and end up enjoying it (no-no to quest to glad gift)!

No-no's can also transit directly to glad gifts via positive associations, though it takes time. I began to enjoy at least playing (versus teaching) tennis a little bit again last summer, when it proved to be about the only way I could get to see tennis-fanatic friends.

Finally, quests can become glad gifts, once learned. Once I learn how to speak Spanish, you probably won't be able to shut me up in that language, either.

Chapter 4: Satisfying Work for Volunteers

So, go with the flow. Remember, too, that surrounding your window is a veritable galaxy of neutral activities, neither glad gifts, nor quests, nor no-no's. Sometimes, the flow becomes a kind of vortex sucking them into the window in any of its three parts. Conversely, anything now in the window might spin off and out into neutral limbo.

Going from the Window to the Right Work

Suppose we have windows now for both prospective and present volunteers. How do we move from this motivational data base to the "solution": the most appropriate work for the volunteer? First of all, I hope the volunteer will be encouraged to participate actively throughout the process.

The challenge is to build together work which:

1. Taps into at least one or two of the individual's Glad Gifts. However, you shouldn't expect to be able to involve all or most of a person's glad gifts. These rarely form a single coherent pattern, in any case, as our sample windows indicate.

2. Provides growth opportunities in at least one Quest area.

3. Avoids all No-No's, or at the very least compensates carefully for any unavoidable aversions.

4. Can be accomplished within the time the person has to invest. Time available information comes from sources other than the window. However, the window might influence this factor. Thus, most people can find a lot more time for glad gifts than no-no's; they'll make more time for what they like to do and want to learn. Conversely, assignment of no-no's encourages people to remember how little time they have.

5. Be of clear, present, and important use to the organization or agency. The window process can easily tempt design of work only to please the worker. Wrong. The work must please both worker and worked for. Volunteer assignments must be designed to help the organization as well as to please the volunteer, just as we have discussed in the preceding chapter on staff Job Factors: the volunteer's Window of Work should fit the staff's "door of opportunity."

A reasonably complete window of work, processed in terms of the foregoing five criteria, will yield at least fifty distinct volunteer job possibilities. Try it with the window examples presented here. My own window (Figure 2) has generated over 100 appropriate volunteer job possibilities for me; several of which I've happily filled in recent years.

Ordinarily, only a really rigid organization fails to find something it can build around a person's reasonably complete Window of Work. Even when an organization, intent on slow suicide in the increasingly fierce competition for volunteers, restricts itself to just one or two roles for volunteers, the window can still suggest how a volunteer can best fill that role; e.g., what kind of a case aide, office worker, etc.

Building Staff/Volunteer Relations © 2003 Energize, Inc.

Chapter 4: Satisfying Work for Volunteers

I've tried window-type job building with hundreds of people and have come to this firm conclusion: there's no such thing as an apathetic person; there are only unimaginative interviewers working with incomplete information for inflexible organizations. Particularly in such cases, the window can be used at the volunteer's rather than the organization's initiative, in the search for meaningful work.

Other Windows, Other Rooms

This chapter is oriented to placing volunteers productively and happily in work via the window. There are also a number of other possible uses, less explored at present. Among these are:

1. Exchange windows with a friend, spouse, co-worker, partner, family member, etc. Discuss. Have you, out of ignorance, been playing too much to each other's no-no's, neglecting each other's glad gifts, and forgetting to give the other person enough chances for growth (quests)?

2. As a paid person or volunteer, see if your boss at work is willing to look at your window, the better to motivate you and use your potential.

3. You as a boss, get and use windows with people you supervise.

4. Use your window as a way of monitoring satisfaction in your present volunteer and/or paid job. Are there still enough glad gifts in it? At least a few opportunities for growth (quests)? Has the job come to require too many no-no's for you? About every six months I take out my window of work, retouch it as necessary, and use it to gauge the level of fulfillment in my current work situations, paid or volunteer.

5. If the above kind of analysis shows a serious lack of fulfillment in your present job, use the window to visualize the kind of job you should be looking for, the job which would maximize chances to use glad gifts, seek quests, and minimize no-no's.

6. Options 4 and 5 above might also apply to other parts of your life; for example, homelife, leisure time, marriage, relationships, family.

7. What about preparing windows for organizations? Glad gifts would translate to something like "willingly shared resources or competencies." Quests and no-no's would remain pretty much as with an individual. Even for small and struggling organizations, composite windows are enormously impressive and illuminating.

The Window of Work has many uses. Let the light shine through.

Building Staff/Volunteer Relations © 2003 Energize, Inc.

Connecting the Window of Work and the Job Factor Processes

Having enabled employees and volunteers to analyze their work and preferences, we can now compare staff Job Factor need lists (X + T + D + Q) with volunteer Work Windows in a number of different ways. The possible variations are:

1. A combined staff "work assistance need list" is reviewed in relation to available volunteer Work Windows. Reviewer is the coordinator or other volunteer program leadership person.

2. Ditto, review of individual staff "work assistance need" lists.

3. The combined staff work assistance needs list is circulated to present or potential volunteers who compare it to their work windows.

4. Ditto, the work assistance need list is circulated to volunteers separately for individual staff/gatekeepers.

5. A group of staff/gatekeepers and volunteers exchange Job Factors and Work Windows and discuss them face-to-face, with a view to making matches.

6. A combined volunteer Work Window is circulated to individual staff who each compare it to their own Job Factor need list.

7. Ditto, individual volunteer Work Windows are circulated to staff to compare with their Job Factors.

8. In the future, I can visualize a variation in which each participant enters the process as both giver and receiver of help, which is to say with both a Job Factor and a Work Window. Each participant then scans all other Job Factors relative to her/his own Window while all other participants review her/his Job Factor in relation to their Windows of Work. The result should be a more fulfilling and effective redistribution of tasks among staff among volunteers, or any combination.

However many matches are made in the above ways, we must always remember that a single spinoff, team or dream, doesn't always correspond exactly to a volunteer job. Various combinations and permutations may still have to be made. For example, a spinoff sweetened by a dream, or a dream shared among several dream-implementers.

At long last, then, we come to the volunteer job description. This occurs, please note, at the end of the volunteer job development process, not at the beginning as some seem to think. Job descriptions are simply the record of that process, not an influence in it. And because Job Factors change, as do Work Windows, I suggest you do each at least twice a year. This means that volunteer job descriptions should not be engraved on tablets of stone. Instead, write them in slowly disappearing ink.

Chapter 4: Satisfying Work for Volunteers

Interlude on Empowerment

An important way of empowering people is to give them work which fits their talents, is sensitive to their needs for growth, and is meaningful in terms of their values. In that sense, this and the preceding chapter are about empowerment through work—first for staff and then for volunteers.

I believe genuinely empowered people are more likely to be comfortable about sharing power in cooperative endeavors. I therefore think empowering both volunteers and staff in their work empowers teamwork at the same time.

In all these ways, the agency overall will be empowered and, one hopes, all its clients.

Chapter 4: Satisfying Work for Volunteers

Building the Team

By applying the Job Factor and Window of Work techniques, staff will come to realize they have choices on what volunteers will do—a wide range of choices. Try to help them make these choices in a way which assures a feeling of ownership in the volunteer program. Because staff won't support *your* program. Why should they?

They will support *their* program and the formula for that is:

participation = ownership = support

So, volunteer coordinator, while you're preaching to staff about how they ought to delegate to volunteers, practice a little delegation yourself—to staff. The checklist on the following page and the instructions below will help you organize the process.

1. Complete the checklist on the next page for your volunteer program, indicating the level of staff participation in major volunteer program functions. Rate each function on a scale of 1 = no participation at all, through 5 = perfect or complete staff participation.

2. Place a checkmark (✓) next to the program functions in which staff participation is relatively lower.

3. Circle those checked items for which it seems most feasible to implement a significantly higher level of staff participation.

4. Outline strategies for doing this (action plan) for at least some of the circled items.

5. List some of the main barriers to developing more staff participation/ownership. How might these barriers relate to some of the other principles for winning with staff discussed elsewhere in this book?

If you, as a volunteer program leader, cannot delegate significant participation effectively to staff, you are a main contributor to staff/volunteer difficulties. Among other things, you are allowing management and staff to dump all volunteer program responsibility on you. Let the volunteer coordinator's Job Factor (Figure 1 in Chapter 3) be an inspiration to you.

Chapter 5: Building the Team

```
                                              Staffing Participation Level
                                              Rate (low) 1, 2, 3, 4, or 5 (high)
Volunteer Program Planning ............................... (  )
Volunteer Job Design ...................................... (  )
Recruiting ................................................. (  )
Screening/Matching ....................................... (  )
Pre-Service Training of Volunteers ......................... (  )
In-Service Training of Volunteers .......................... (  )
Supervision/Evaluation of Volunteers ...................... (  )
Program-level Assessment/Evaluation ...................... (  )
Recognition of Volunteers ................................. (  )
Public Relations ........................................... (  )
                                                    TOTAL = [   ]
```

Doubling the total gives a staff participation index ranging from a low of 20 to a high of 100. Anything below 35-40 should be considered a seriously low staff participation level in your volunteer program.

For Whom Is the Program?

It may be time to reconsider phrases such as "volunteer program" as the only way of presenting ourselves. The growing suspicion is that the labeling suggests an incomplete or distorted view of who the program is for and how widely important it is.

Let's look at labeling, first from the point of view of who the program is for.

For whom is a latchkey program? Latchkey children, right?

For whom is a victim assistance program? Victims, of course.

For whom is a volunteer program? Volunteers? It sounds like it, when in fact we want the volunteer program primarily to serve staff and clients.

Another pressure for name change is the need for titles to refer more to outcomes achieved than to who is achieving them (volunteers).

As for outcomes, they often are far broader, actually, than the services rendered by volunteers. Studies conducted by the Center for Creative Community suggest that almost three-quarters of volunteer coordinators spend a significant to substantial amount of worktime doing other things besides volunteer program coordination. That "something else" frequently centers on what is better called "community resource mobilization," with volunteers as just one part of that.

Other community contributions in that package include materials (clothing, food, etc.), facilities, equipment, information, ideas, feedback, support, advocacy, and money. It is increasingly credible to see these various avenues of community contribution not as separates, but rather as part of a single integrated whole called "community resources," or some such name.

Building Staff/Volunteer Relations © 2003 Energize, Inc.

As but one example, there is evidence that people who give time to a cause (volunteers) are more than averagely likely also to give money to that cause. For others, increased awareness of the full range of options in giving makes it more likely they will find a congenial one, e.g., materials if not time, or vice versa. From the staff perspective, this presents a far wider and more attractive range of potential options for enhancing their job satisfaction and effectiveness (Chapter 3 on job factoring).

In this view, trying to get staff support for volunteer services as a solo separate is something like trying to ride a unicycle. You have to be an acrobat to manage such an inherently unstable vehicle. We could instead be riding a far more stable four- (or more) wheeled vehicle, by presenting ourselves as orchestrators of all the various kinds of community contributions described above. In other words, the perception many now have of us as an expendable "luxury" is due to an overly narrow packaging of what we really are and do.

The frequently more appropriate, and always more defensible, perception would be symbolized by moving from names like "volunteer program" to broader titles. Thus the staff or executive who might have a patronizing attitude toward the volunteer program as a frill will have a harder time taking the same attitude towards a "community-based support system," or "community resource development program," or a "community relations division."

Consider it just a much larger umbrella to keep the rain off. Many apparently do, for the popularity of these new, broader titles is steadily growing among those who formerly called themselves "volunteer coordinator," "director of volunteer services," or the like. Until management is ready to embrace the broader title, keep it as a surreptitious alternate (and don't tell anyone I suggested it).

For those who worry that this abandons the volunteer, I'd argue, first of all, that volunteer programs will have far more opportunity to survive, and thrive, *with staff support*, as part of an integrated community resource mobilization program. Moreover the volunteer identification can still be preserved and cherished as an alternative title in a large part of your program and in all of your heart.

Communicating...for Togetherness

I believe it was Justice Brandeis who said: "Sunlight is the best disinfectant." Surely that applies to infections in the partnership between staff and volunteers. Put otherwise, imprecision and isolation breed paranoia, and good communication is the cure. The trouble is, ideal ongoing communication between staff and volunteers probably would take more time than either realistically ought to give it. It makes little sense for a volunteer, in the office only two hours a week, to spend one hour perfecting communication techniques with staff. It makes even less sense for a staff person supervising fifty volunteers to spend fifty hours per week communicating with them. We're all supposed to be working together most of the time, not "resolving problems" in our relationship.

What we need is a kind of economical, representative communication which does the job, taking as little time as possible away from staff or volunteer work. The idea is to get enough sunlight without leaving home to live on the Equator.

One suggestion is to have well-thought-out job descriptions which staff and volunteers participate in developing. These will serve as a kind of crystallized communication, as clear benchmarks or reference points for discussing the work volunteers do (see Chapters 3 and 4).

Another recommendation is to develop processes in which focused, intensive communication among a sample of volunteers and staff stand for or represent the less organized, more time-consuming communication which would otherwise be necessary.

A classic representative communication model is an advisory council of volunteers "speaking for" all volunteers in the program. Similarly, a staff committee may represent other staff; or a mixed staff/volunteer group speak for both.

Here's a more recently developed representative communication model which has proven effective. It takes as little as 45 minutes, and requires as few as three or four each of volunteers and staff. The process can encompass as many as 25 of each but should then limit sub-group size to six to eight people. Here's an outline of the model:

1. The "bouquet bounce." Small group(s) of volunteers brainstorm a list of all the things they like about staff. NO PROBLEMS PERMITTED, at this point. Staff group(s) at the same time list all the things they like about volunteers. Then share both lists publicly, lavishly, lovingly. Bask, don't rush.

   There are some very moving moments here, especially when wonderful surprises turn up of the type: "Gosh, we didn't know you liked that about us." By contrast, communication usually plunges immediately into problems, creating a grimly pessimistic climate which may overwhelm problem-solving. So, let's get the glow first. You'll be surprised how long it will continue to light the way to later problem-solving.

2. Now, mixed small groups of staff and volunteers work up lists of "what we need to work on together." The advantage is that issues are reality-tested within the mixed group, and come out as consensus statements rather than "charges" hurled at staff by volunteers, or vice versa. Interestingly enough, many problems surfacing at this point prove to be not so much issues between staff and volunteers as general administrative concerns affecting both. Thus, when volunteers in a mental institution requested "patient highlight summaries" for quick orientation during occasional visits, staff response was: "Heck, we'd like that, too. Let's both talk to administration about it."

3. Disseminate the step 1 and 2 results widely in newsletters, meetings, reports, etc.

4. Follow up on consensus concerns expressed in step 2 (maybe a joint committee of participants could be involved here). Report back on results.

5. Repeat the process about once every six months, possibly with a partly different group of volunteers and staff.

Stay in touch without taking all your time to do it.

We tend to concentrate on instances of discrimination against volunteers—which do exist. We need also to consider the case in which volunteers get better treatment than staff higher quality training, more careful matching to appropriate work, and above all, more recognition. Small wonder staff are sometimes envious.

Chapter 5: Building the Team

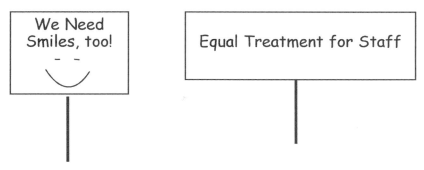

The remedy is more sensitive equalizing of benefits. If, for example, volunteers have better on-site training than staff—as often happens—the volunteer coordinator should at least offer to share relevant parts of that training with staff. Certainly, before advocating additional training for volunteers, the coordinator should first support more training for staff.

The gap is most glaring in regard to appreciation and recognition. Here are the crucial intangible rewards which the psychologist Herzberg long ago noted can be as important to employees as money. I've confirmed this on numerous occasions by presenting lists of recommended volunteer recognitions to paid staff and asking them if they'd also like to have such smiles, thanks, pats on the back, etc. The answer, of course, is a near-unanimous YES. Being paid doesn't disqualify people from needing and deserving appreciation.

Generally, a good volunteer program models the kind of humane, effective leadership which is the right of all workers. Suddenly, staff get their noses rubbed in the fact that they are not being treated that way and—to add insult to injury—must nevertheless extend themselves to treat volunteers that way. Unconsciously or not, in such a situation, staff are prone to resent "teacher's pet" volunteers.

This situation gives rise to the famous "principle of positive confusion": Don't just treat volunteers as if they were staff; treat staff as if they were volunteers! Each equally has the right to respect for ability and extra-mile effort; each needs intangible rewards, good training, and supervision, and work which is fulfilling. Compound this benevolent confusion by:

~ Trying always to recognize volunteer/staff teams rather than just volunteers alone.

~ Recognizing staff for volunteer work they do elsewhere in the community. (Though be sensitive if some staff feel that is their private business.)

~ Where possible, recognizing staff for a "volunteer attitude" towards their work in the agency/organization.

~ Overall, being the visible advocate of deserving staff getting the same kinds of "psychological paychecks" as do volunteers. Because staff need it as much as volunteers—maybe more—and the volunteer program is likely to get support mainly from generally fulfilled staff.

To repeat, the volunteer program can get just so far out front in the effective humanizing of work, before staff begin to feel the pain of the difference, and perhaps pass on that pain to volunteers. Therefore, what we are—and must be—is apostles of humanity in the workplace.

For all workers, not just for a privileged few.

A Search for Common Ground

Volunteers are special people. The trouble is, in our enthusiasm for telling people just how special they are, we end up segregating them. This apartheid-by-appreciation does no one any good. In fact, it is the entering wedge for alienation and conflict between staff and volunteers. By contrast, we should support the single-species theory which holds that staff and volunteers belong to the same human race:

~ They often sit next to each other in church or synagogue.

~ Their kids go to the same schools...they live in the same neighborhoods.

~ They belong to many of the same clubs.

~ Mostly, they each care deeply about the organization they work for and its mission.

~ It has been demonstrated repeatedly that volunteers and staff can intermarry and produce offspring.

So there! Whatever anyone tells you, volunteers did not just get off the ship from Mars.

You wouldn't guess it from what we often say—or imply—about volunteers. Some "seeming separators," dramatized a bit for effect, are:

~ We have two kinds of people in this agency. Staff people and volunteer people. You know they're different because they have different training, supervision, recognition, etc. We even have a specialist "volunteer coordinator" to work with those different volunteer people.

~ You know volunteers care because they're unpaid. On the other hand, staff who are paid,_____(don't care?).

~ Volunteers, because they're unpaid, need intangible rewards. Staff because they're paid, do not. (We just dealt with that.)

~ Staff are professionals. Volunteers, on the other hand, are_____(not professionals?).

~ Volunteers tend to be rich, idle ladies. Staff on the other hand are____(poor, busy, males?).

~ We expect excellence from our staff. From volunteers, we pretty much take what we can get.

~ You can fire staff but you can't fire volunteers, no matter what they do.

BOSH! The last two points, dealt with already, need only be touched on here. Any rational organization expects the best from all its workers, paid or unpaid, and reserves the right to terminate the employment of people who don't measure up.

The professional versus non-professional barrier crumbles on even cursory examination. An estimated 15% of all volunteers are professionals serving as volunteers in their professional capacity: accountants, doctors, attorneys, public relations professionals, dentists, nurses, social workers, psychologists, and on and on. Conversely, many paid staff do not have professional education.

Surveys increasingly give the lie to all the other alleged demographic differences, such as "all volunteers are women." In North America, at least, the profile of volunteers has come to substantially resemble the profile of all people. This is one reason the search for the profile of the "typical volunteer" drives me up the wall. Volunteers are, or should be, every man and every woman—every person. Beyond that, obsession with special profiles, maybe special genes too, unnecessarily narrows our recruiting focus, and perpetuates the myth of a helping elite. The same energy could better be applied to increasing the accessibility of volunteering to all people.

The bit about volunteers caring because they're unpaid is the unkindest cut of all to staff persons. Their resentment of it is perfectly understandable. An underpaid staff person who hangs in there 40 hours a week (in contrast to the volunteer's two hours) has got to care, at some level—or once did before becoming a casualty of the system. In my book, any caring that staff person shows, in spite of the daily, weekly and yearly batterings of time, is heroic.

Finally, when we behave as if we have two "types" of people at the agency—volunteer types and staff types—are we being realistic? I think not. Surveys consistently suggest that about half of all Americans volunteer. That means something like half of all the agency's staff people probably volunteer somewhere else in town (and ought to be recognized for it).

On the other side, almost two-thirds of today's volunteers are also paid employees of some other organization. Most of the rest have worked for money at some time in their lives.

The point is, we all understand what it is to be a paid employee, and at the same time, we're all part of the volunteer family. Most of us have some experience with both work-statuses. The overlap is even more pronounced when we adopt the broadest (and to me most meaningful) definition of volunteering: doing more than you have to because you want to, in a cause you consider good. I sometimes use that definition with a group of staff who may be a little uncomfortable about a planned new volunteer program. Then I say:

Hear this list through and raise your hand at the end if you've done any of these things. Have you ever:

~ written a letter to the editor?

~ comforted a crying child?

~ voted?

~ given someone directions on the street?

Chapter 5: Building the Team

~ helped out a sick neighbor?

~ belonged to a service club?

~ belonged to a religious congregation?

~ held a door open for someone entering or leaving a building behind you?

~ tried to cheer up a friend who was having a hard time?

By the way, how much were you paid for it? And did anybody force you to do it?

In any case, at the end of such a discussion all or virtually all staff hands go up, and we can begin to talk about volunteering as an experience we all share in one form or another. ("...And how do you like to be treated when you volunteer?")

The counterpart exercise with volunteers is to identify and discuss their past or present experiences as paid employees. If not their own experiences, those of someone close to them.

Where separatism persists, however, the danger remains of slipping into a competitive approach. This happens most obviously in research or evaluation which compares volunteers versus staff doing essentially the same job. Whoever "wins" on that, both lose. Beyond formal evaluation, everyday conversation and communication must be careful to quash the competitive. Watch, too, the comparison (in at least one famous early research) which showed volunteers doing a great job in a setting where there had never been staff before. What this seems to imply is that we'll never need staff in this setting. That could be true, in some cases, but I'd certainly want to hold off on signaling that implication, 'til we're sure.

The comparison we always want to make is:

staff alone… vs… staff *plus* volunteers

Thus, it's not that volunteers can conduct public relations as well as or better than staff. Rather, it's that a team of staff and volunteers can do a much better job than staff alone, or volunteers alone, for that matter. It's the difference between comparing Dick versus Jane as individuals, on the one hand, in contrast to noting that Dick and Jane together seem to do better than either alone. Which kind of comparison would be more supportive of their marriage?

Speaking of getting along together, maybe it's time to go back and have a talk with Frank Miller….

Building Staff/Volunteer Relations © 2003 Energize, Inc.

Afterword

'Til We Meet Again: Afterword from the 1987 Edition

Don't expect another sequel to this book in another ten years; things will be settled long before that, I think.

If the strategies presented here are seriously tried, I believe there's an excellent chance they will work. Then we'll have more than a few tantalizing exceptions to the rule that a genuine general partnership between staff and volunteers is an unattainable dream, after 30 years or more.

At least equally probable, I fear, is a worst-case scenario which may already have begun. The volunteer effort in human service agencies becomes a steadily ossifying foothold (or toehold). It becomes institutionalized as a tame self-congratulating token of what genuine community involvement might have meant in humanizing human services, and in adding a special dimension of creativity to it.

The vital energies of volunteering seek other less blocked outlets, among them the group composed entirely of volunteers (an estimated six million of them in America); independent freelance volunteering; the informal non-program volunteering of every day life; and the application of volunteer leadership principles to paid employment. There are signs even today of more movement to and through these more open gates to participation in a free society. I further sense the outlines of exciting new careers based on these alternative channels for volunteering.

It's nearly our last chance to win with staff.

Or they with us.

Now That We've Met Again *(Let's Start Getting Ready for Next Time)*

"'Til We Meet Again" concluded the previous edition of this book, some five years ago. Projected there were three possible predictions for the future of staff/volunteer relations. A fourth "scenario" has evolved since then, and I'd like to consider all four in this afterword: The Final Success Scenario; The Stagnation Scenario; The Migration Scenario; and the Transformation Scenario.

The Final Success Scenario

"'Til We Meet Again" predicted that "... things will be settled long before [ten years hence]... if the strategies here are seriously tried." Wrong on both counts. Overall, staff/volunteer relations are far from satisfactorily "settled." Moreover, I believe our proposed strategies have not yet become the mainstream choice in volunteer administration, and may never be so. True, this book continues to have a somewhat ominous popularity (ominous because if the book were completely successful, it would no longer be necessary). In any case, we have not reached the end of history for the problem of staff/volunteer relations.

The Stagnation Scenario

Another quote from five years ago: "The volunteer effort in human service agencies [will become] a steadily ossifying foothold.. .a token of what community involvement might have meant." This scenario may already have come true. In many quarters, implacable rigidities persist in our approach to staff/volunteer relations, e.g., if there's a problem, escalate praise of volunteers and treat staff skepticism as neuroticism rather than realism.

On the other hand, I sense some movement, mainly in recognition that organizational as well as individual responsibility must be taken to ensure the success of volunteer programs. This movement is all the more remarkable in light of volunteerism's traditional faith in the power of the individual to handle just about anything. (We've always been more congenial to psychology than sociology.)

This explains the historically dominant assumption that the volunteer coordinator will pretty much do it all alone. That theory still holds in much of the present book. For example, the individual volunteer coordinator has primary responsibility for seeing that Windows of Work and Job Factors are taken and sensitively matched, that volunteer training emphasizes respect for staff and vice versa, etc.

But this book also begins to recognize organization-wide responsibility for the success of a volunteer program, especially at the executive level, and especially in the formulation and implementation of positive volunteer program policies. Susan J. Ellis' book, *From the Top Down* (Energize, 1996), has given powerful impetus to this movement.

Beyond the individual (volunteer coordinator) and the single host organization (especially its top management), there is an even "higher" level of responsibility: that of the volunteer community as a whole, represented by Volunteer Centers, DOVIAs or other concerned collections of individuals or agencies. This is beginning to happen and I hope/predict it will happen even more in the years ahead. Very briefly, examples include Volunteer Coordinator of the Year awards by professional associations, raising prestige for all of us. Or, a few brilliant Volunteer Centers reward agencies for treating their volunteers well (or at least not abusing them too obviously). The latter is a carrot, not a stick, approach, although we can't help it if questions are asked about agencies who did not get an award.

Who knows? Someday the volunteer community may sponsor Volunteer Week events which, instead of implying how easily dedicated volunteers can be taken for granted, suggest just the opposite. How about "Volunteers Take a Day Off"? An hour, perhaps? Ten minutes, maybe? The upper boundary of possibility here is somewhere between our need to keep our jobs and our need to have everybody like us.

The Migration Scenario

From five years ago, this prediction: "The vital energies of volunteering seek other less blocked exits, among them the group composed entirely of volunteers...." (The blockage here is understood to be in agency volunteer programs.)

Could be. At least, the stage is being set for such a migration. First of all, a solid knowledge base is being established for the effective operation of entirely-volunteer

Afterword

groups. Energize, Inc. has uniquely begun to devote a section of its Web site (www.energizeinc.com) and Online Bookstore to this major component of the volunteer community, including my book: *When Everyone's a Volunteer: The Effective Functioning of All-Volunteer Groups* (Energize, 1992). Application of all this knowledge will make all-volunteer groups a more attractive option for volunteers, that is, make the predicted migration more likely. (Though, in fairness, it is important to recognize that the interrelationships of volunteers with one another, particularly long-time members and newcomers, can be as complicated as anything that occurs between employees and volunteers!)

Also adding to the attractiveness of the entirely-volunteer option for volunteers is the increasing likelihood of accessible professional assistance for such groups. Initial study suggests that a role such as "Consultant to All-Volunteer Groups" will evolve as a viable career alternative for today's volunteer coordinators. A career incubation project, now underway, will have more to report on this in a year or two.

Let us then suppose the gates are opening for an out-migration of volunteers from agency volunteer programs towards entirely-volunteer groups. Will such a prospect cause agencies to treat their volunteers better, and their volunteer coordinators, too? Possibly, in some cases. But agencies which never deeply valued their volunteers anyhow, won't fight to keep them.

The Transformation Scenario

The staff/volunteer problem will be transformed before it is solved. The transformation, very simply stated, will be from a one-part to a three-part problem. Where heretofore we have seen ourselves dealing only with volunteers' relation to staff, now we will be dealing with all possible interactions between volunteers, staff, and mandated community service workers (alternative service offenders, obligated service for youth, etc.).

There are three interactions to deal with: the traditional one between volunteers and staff, plus additional interactions between mandated service people and volunteers, and mandated service participants and staff. I only hope we'll do some serious study of the last two relationships before we get unpleasantly surprised by some of their ramifications.

Thus, it's likely volunteers will increasingly be working side-by-side with mandated service workers, sometimes doing the same or similar things. Are positive mentor-type linkups possible? Will some volunteers lose their taste for choosing to do what other people are ordered to do—and even partly paid to do?

Is there a type of staff person who's very uncomfortable because volunteers need to be persuaded and motivated? Wouldn't such a staff person therefore prefer mandated workers who, presumably, don't have to be persuaded and motivated? Are there entire agencies that feel that way?

Farewell. My only firm prediction is that we'll never run out of questions.

2003 Update

A new century—the same issues. In reviewing this book once again, it is clear that the relationships between volunteers and employees are still too often problematic. But all the reasons for creating the best teamwork possible are as pertinent today as they always were. Become an in-house educator and reap the rewards!

Building Staff/Volunteer Relations © 2003 Energize, Inc.

Afterword

Appendix A

A Starting Point for Policy Formation about Volunteers

There is wide agreement that articulating policies about volunteer involvement in an agency is highly desirable—but the policies need to be in writing, carefully considered, and regularly reconsidered. Below are some subject areas which are suggested frequently as needing policy determination. The exact wording is, of course, up to each individual organization. Note, too, that as policy, the statement does not intend to cover details of volunteer program implementation.

~ There is a statement about the commitment to volunteer involvement in service delivery in the organization's mission statement.

~ With every prospective new staff member, we explore and expect a positive or at least an open-minded attitude toward volunteers and related community resource development.

~ In every staff job description, there is a strong statement to the effect that volunteers are one important way to get things done, etc.

~ Serious orientation to volunteers is part of every new staff member's orientation to the agency. The Volunteer Coordinator does this part of the orientation.

~ In-service training for staff provides the skill development necessary to supervise and liaison with volunteers on a continuing basis.

~ All staff are expected to develop meaningful assignments for volunteers.

~ There are definite incentive/rewards for staff who work well with volunteers.

~ "How are you doing involving the community?" is the kind of question asked of every staff member at every performance evaluation.

~ Each top management person shall model the agency's commitment to volunteers by recruiting and supervising at least one volunteer.

~ Affirmative action policy and values apply equally to the volunteer program.

~ Volunteers are held to performance standards, are evaluated on a periodic basis, and can be reassigned or terminated for poor performance.

Building Staff/Volunteer Relations

Appendix A

~ We consider volunteer involvement "real work" and will provide references for paid employment, college applications, etc. for deserving volunteers on that basis.

~ Volunteer work in the agency does not in any way preclude a person's full consideration for paid employment in our agency. On the other hand, it does not guarantee such employment.

~ Clear and effective grievance procedures will be open to both volunteers and staff on matters that may need to be resolved between them, or between either and the agency.

~ Wherever possible, volunteers shall be treated as staff.

~ Wherever possible, staff shall be treated with all the consideration given to volunteers.

Policy statements need some "teeth" in them. Consider the following example from the Texas Department of Mental Health and Mental Retardation (MHMR). "The Rules of the Commissioner of MHMR Governing the Internal Management of Facilities of the Department 302.05.03.020-(O) (Rev. 9/1/81)":

The use of volunteers shall be a consideration in determining merit pay increases if the use of volunteers is feasible and they are available at the work location and the employee has the authority to request volunteers.

Appendix B

"Titles of Caring":
An Exercise to Expand the Concept of Volunteer Involvement

The preceding pages have suggested a number of techniques for helping staff to consider their own jobs and the work that volunteers might do. The following is yet another approach to encourage staff involvement and to confront stereotypes on the limited kinds of things volunteers can do. The goal is to show staff that volunteers *expand staff's range of choices*, rather than limit them.

Step 1.
Look at the "All People Everywhere in All Ways Are Volunteers" list* on the following page, which contains more than 150 different volunteer job titles, in a wide range of activities. Either use this as a handout or prepare your own local list, being sure you know what each of the volunteer job titles means. Your local Volunteer Center, RSVP, or professional association (DOVIA) can help you develop this list.

Step 2.
Distribute the list to staff. As a warm-up, they get a chance to challenge you on the meaning of any of the intriguing job titles and also ask: "Do volunteers actually do that?" "Where?" There should be a few relaxing laughs along with concept-expanding insights here.

Step 3.
Brainstorm "Titles of Caring" related to your helping effort or organization. Often people are amazed at the number of good things happening they just hadn't thought about or had somehow taken for granted. This step helps ensure that we take account of all the volunteer contributions which are actually occurring (whether the word "volunteer" is used or not). Further, it alerts us to the possibility of giving people recognition for some of this heretofore secret volunteering and, in this way and other ways, helps cultivate more of it.

Step 4.
Now go back over the list in step 3 and see if you can think of any more attractive (though still accurate) names for the things volunteers do. In some cases this might simply be a "catchier" title. (While I might agree to your "gardener's aide," somehow I'd be even more enthusiastic about being one of your "Green Guerrillas"!) In other cases, the alternative suggested name for something volunteers do might simply ensure fuller recognition of the dignity and importance of the work.

Building Staff/Volunteer Relations © 2003 Energize, Inc.

Afterword | **Appendix B**

Step 5.
Now brainstorm a separate list of names of things people might do voluntarily for your helping effort, but aren't doing as yet. This future "Honor Roll" can be the starting point for opening up fresh channels of service, and at the same time involving more people in your work.

Step 6.
Maybe the future ideas can be represented visually in some imaginative and attractive way, as in the figure below. Such visuals can be put up on posters or newsprint in high traffic areas for staff or volunteers to add to at will.

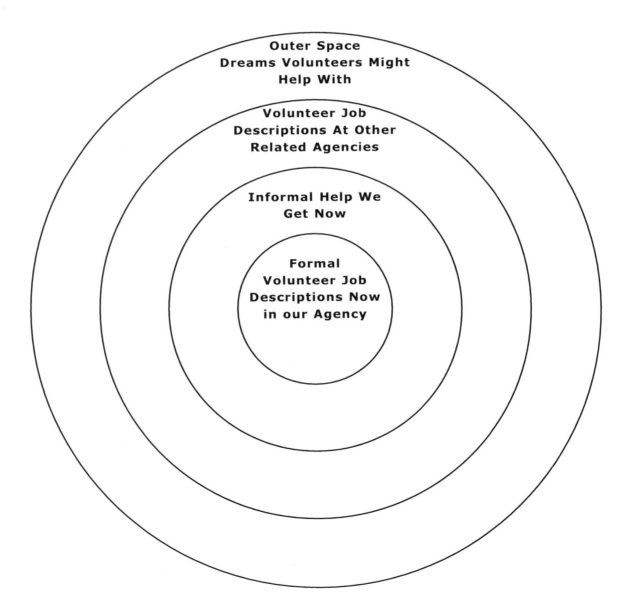

Building Staff/Volunteer Relations © 2003 Energize, Inc.

Appendix B Afterword

All People Everywhere in All Ways are VOLUNTEERS*

*weather watchers • loaned executives • library storytellers • veterans' rights educators • CB emergency monitors • coaches for youth teams • archeological diggers • one-to-one companions • union shop stewards • police reservists • cookie bakers • disaster relief workers • aluminum can recyders • blood donors • symphony supporters • docents • parliamentarians • altar guild members • student government-officers • refugee sponsors • car poolers • bike path advocates • parade marchers • garden therapy aides • activists • swim meet officials • donations picker-uppers • neighborhood organizers • consultants to minority-business • scorekeepers • telethon phone-answerers • puppeteers • host families • free-clinic doctors • typists • career role models • protestors • wood choppers • handbook authors • broadcast license-reviewers • telephone reassurance-callers • Christmas carollers • snowmobile trail breakers • hospice counselors • animal shelter assistants • job developers • flood level monitors • UFO sighting recorders • umpires • food co-op helpers • staplers • postal stamp design-advisors • class parents • paper drive organizers • resource finders • political precinct-canvassers • trial crew coordinators • historic preservers • tutors • alternative school initiators • space colony planners • downtown revitalizers • boothworkers • greeting card senders • troop leaders • convention delegates • ham radio operators • anti-vivisectiontets • "safe house" families • tenants union organizers • sorority/fraternity advisors • fishing partners • safety marshalls • newsletter collators • bazaar chairpeople • school safety patrolers • litter picker-uppers • income tax preparers • handbell choir members • youth club leaders • swimming buddies • eligibility interviewers • thrift shop salespeople • foster parents • boycotters • scholarship developers • ushers • conservationists • golf tournament-organizers • teen jury members • braille transcribers • ambulance drivers • grant writers • college trustees • hotline managers • barter traders • immunization-campaigners • survey respondents • leaf rakers • Sunday School teachers club coordinators • patient advocates • emergency shelter-providers • deacons • civil defense coordinators • wheelchair ramp builders • poll workers • tennis linesmen/ women • mountain search and rescue members • "huggers" • town officials • dentist appointment-hand-holders • fundraisers • playground helpers • mainstreamers • barn tenders • skill sharers • choir leaders • family planning counselors • community theater crews• gleaners • mentors • soup makers and takers • vision screeners • firefighters • court watchers • poison prevention-educators • lobbyists • crisis counselors • commissioners • floating checkpoint-coordinators • greeters • letter-to-the-editor writers • marathon-for-charity-runners • clean-up workers • trail markers • board members • community festival-workers • geneology researchers • house sitters • student interns • interpreters • ticket sellers • steering committee-members • corrections advocates • friendly visitors • acolyte coordinators • community architects • solar insolation monitors • classroom assistants • donators• speakers • bureau-members• consumer advocates • child-minders • nursing-home visitors • letter-writers for patients • legal advisors • patterning instructors • bookmobile staffers • crime watch patrollers • peacemakers

*Originally a poster published by Energize Inc. in 1981, based on my earlier "Titles of Caring." We encouraged people to "keep the list growing."

Building Staff/Volunteer Relations © 2003 Energize, Inc.

Made in the USA
Lexington, KY
11 January 2015